Why I Follow Jesus

Why I Follow Jesus

Adrian Plass

Marshall Pickering
An Imprint of HarperCollinsPublishers

Marshall Pickering is an Imprint of
HarperCollins*Religious*
Part of HarperCollins*Publishers*
77–85 Fulham Palace Road, London W6 8JB
www.christian-publishing.com

First published in Great Britain in 2000
by HarperCollins*Religious*

3 5 7 9 10 8 6 4 2

A catalogue record for this book is
available from the British Library

ISBN 0 551 03112 3

Printed and bound in Great Britain by
Omnia Books Limited, Glasgow

DEDICATION

My job involves meeting and listening to lots of people. Sometimes I feel overwhelmed by the sheer volume of folk who battle continually with deep hurts and chronic difficulties. When the dark cloud of pain seemed to be blocking out more light than ever, I wrote this poem. If it had come from another age and a different place and had been better written, I suppose it might have been called a psalm.

Winter waking, stretched across the moonstone
  sky,
Caring less than nothing for the destiny of man,
You see the crows, like ragged scraps of dustbin
  bag
Come floating down the wind to scavenge what
  they can,
And nothing need be spoken.
Deep in winter sleep is where you hear the saddest
  cries,
The wheeling dealing seagull souls,
Of men and women taught to stay a step ahead,
Who reached the edge,
But found that when they fell,
They had not learned to fly.
I tell you that it drives you wild,
It drives you out to march and march beside the
  heartless sea,
To weep and rage and beg the only one who really
  knows,

To tell you, tell you, tell you, tell you why,
So many hearts are broken.

This book is dedicated to that special group of people so passionately loved by God the Father – the brokenhearted.

CONTENTS

Why I follow Jesus

Why do I follow Jesus?

It may be foolish to ask this question because, in these pages, I'm planning to answer it truthfully and, although the truth can certainly set us free, it can also cause an awful lot of trouble. Mind you, if I wanted I could avoid trouble by supplying an answer that would be entirely satisfactory to folk who prefer to cement over those cracks that create crazy-paving pathways through the lives of so many of us ordinary believers. Here it is: Christ died and rose again for us, and that act of redemption will save us from an eternity of separation from God, if we sincerely repent of our sins, become baptized and believe in him. *must ?*

There we are. End of book. That is the technical truth of the gospel, a truth I accepted and responded to more than 30 years ago, and I believe it – most of the time. What better motivation is there? None, of course, and yet, that bald statement does not in itself embody the heart of my motivation for following Jesus.

You would think, wouldn't you, that after all these years I might have successfully identified the springs of my faith? It has been quite a long time, you know. I laboriously worked out on a calculator that I have probably attended something like 1,620 church services, plus an equal number of weekday meetings. This means that I have been exposed to the Bible, the gospel and fellow Christians on 3,250 separate occasions – at least! And that's not counting accidental ones on television. Frightening, isn't it? Surely I must have sorted it all out by now? I'm afraid not. It takes so long to learn that you know nothing – or at best, very little.

Why do I continue to follow Jesus? I have burrowed down into the confusion of my feeling and thinking to produce quite a lot of answers for you, and the first one I'm going to mention is, for me anyway, one of the most important.

I follow Jesus because …
I want to be with my friends for ever

Now, this is all very well, but it begs the obvious question, doesn't it? Who *are* my friends? Well, of course, when my thoughts turn in this direction I immediately include my wife, Bridget, and the family, and those close friends who love me and whom I love. Naturally I want to be with all those people who are so important in my life, but there's quite a lot of sorting out to be done in addition to that.

You can see how important this whole area is to Jesus when you read the later chapters in the Gospel of John. Jesus sounds rather like a mother trying to drum into her family that someone must take responsibility for feeding the canary while she's away, or it will die, because she's normally the only one who does it regularly and properly. Over and over and over again he implores the disciples to love one another. We are his friends if we obey his commands, and his command is that we love one another. And that love is to extend, he tells us, not just to those who are close to us and contained within our little corner of his kingdom, but to all Christians, everywhere.

His example is before us – Almighty God, who willingly sent Jesus to be the sorter-out of untied shoelaces. As it happens, Bridget and I know a bit about untied shoelaces. The church often reminds us of the country walks we used to do with children in care when we were residential social workers.

In the front during those memorable walks would be our colleague, Mike, an athlete with huge thighs, no imagination and proper walking equipment, accompanied by his terribly keen support group, all looking like an advert for healthy breakfast cereal.

Next, in the centre, would come me, supervising bright but troubled under-achievers wearing spectacles. We would be whimsically speculating on the poetic, philosophical and artistic significance of hiking.

At the back you would find Bridget, helping the fat ones and the slow ones and the ones whose shoes never stayed done up and the ones with bad feet who didn't believe they were ever going to make it, and the ones who only came because they wanted to get out of doing something else and wished now that they'd put up with whatever it was they'd wanted to avoid.

If you like, the triumphalists were at the front, the liberals in the middle and the servers at the back. I have to be honest and say that my vote goes to the servers every time. In fact, as you know, each group gets annoyed with each of the other groups at one time or another. The triumphalists at the front get annoyed with the group at the back for slowing them down when they want to move on at an even greater pace to even greater heights, and they get annoyed with the group in the middle because they're so unfocused, *abstract* and irrelevant. The servers at the back get annoyed with the triumphalists because they won't *wait*, and seem to want to be a little group all on their own, and they're annoyed with the group in the middle because they seem so *vague* and useless, and the group in the middle get annoyed with anything or anyone that threatens to move them to a position as vulgarly committed as the *front* or the *back.* If only we could swap around from time to time, we might discover some amazing things – not least that the final group will have achieved more than anyone else if they finish the journey, and that will indeed be a mighty triumph!

Just as those children used to squabble and fight, many of us Christians would have to admit, if we are honest, that our enemies are often drawn from among our friends, from the church itself. In certain parts of the world that I have visited, some religious groups are nearer to being enemies than friends. Where that is so, we would do well to remember that Jesus was just as insistent about loving our enemies as loving our friends.

I'm following Jesus because I want to be with my friends, and if I want to be with them in heaven, I've got to be with them now. I've got to own their sins and faults, because even if I don't like them they are friends of a friend, and that friend is Jesus, and he's the friend I most want to be with for ever. This church of ours is his body. Do I love it? How long will it take me finally to pick up my cross and take it to the place of death, to die to my rights and my resentments and my personal agendas, so that, if necessary, I can step out of the group that attracts me, or the mood that I'm in, or the character trait that tries to imprison me, and be what I need to be in the place where I'm most needed?

But it's not only a love for the body of Christ on earth that motivates me to follow. It's Jesus himself. By a miracle of kindness from God himself, I'm allowed to call him my friend. I really do want to be with him for ever.

I follow Jesus because ...
I don't know where else to go and, in any case, I'd find it very hard to stop

Friends of mine who mistakenly fancy themselves as satirists enjoy offering their opinion that the main reasons for my continuing faith are practical and commercial. They suggest that, for someone who makes his living from writing and speaking about the Christian faith, it would be financial suicide publicly to announce my conversion to atheism or the worship of two-toed frogs. Warming to their theme, these alleged f.o.m. further suggest that any virtue I might display is based solely on the awareness that having an affair or committing some other major and visible sin would have a similarly disastrous effect on my career. (This latter theory is, of course, complete nonsense. We've all seen how it's done. Suppose you're a Christian writer who has an affair, for instance. Okay, all you have to do is repent after a decent pause and then write a whole succession of helpful and lucrative books entitled *Picking up the Pieces*, *New Buildings from Old Bricks*, and *God* Will *Forgive You*. A nice little earner, in fact.)

This is all utter rubbish, of course, although I do sometimes wonder if God, in his great wisdom and knowing me so well, has deliberately manoeuvred me into a position where several thousand people can keep an eye on what I'm up to. Who knows?

No, those silly negative reasons for staying with Jesus are as nothing compared with two quite different strands of motivation which, while still apparently negative in nature, are also highly significant.

The first is that I wouldn't know where else to go. Simon Peter, the fishy follower of Jesus, expressed it perfectly in the sixth chapter of John's Gospel. Everyone had been complaining about Jesus' extraordinary claim that he was bread come down from heaven, and that whoever fed on him would live for ever. As many of his disciples turned away and made it mutteringly, grumblingly clear that they no longer wanted to follow him, Jesus turned to his original 12 followers and said, rather plaintively I've always imagined, 'You don't want to leave too, do you?'

'Lord,' said old Simon Peter, 'to whom shall we go? You have the words of eternal life. We believe and know that you are the Holy One of God.'

And it's true, isn't it? We sense that Jesus holds the only available keys to real-life 'happy ever after'. We depend on him knowing the answers to those questions that loom like monsters from the darkness of our inner lives almost from the first moment we discover that death is inevitable. We feel in our bones that he alone can make sure that the narrative of life will have a beginning, a middle *and* a satisfactory end. He's the explanation and solution to the puzzle of why men and women, in their enjoyment and appreciation of theatre and fiction and story, experience a dimension of profound yearning for the clear and rational completeness that characterizes these ancient human pursuits. All of these truths, though dimly perceived much of the time perhaps, shine like beacons to the lost child inside us, making it very difficult, if not impossible, to do anything but hang around waiting to see where he will lead us next. Every road except his, however dangerously long, and however alluring, is a cul-de-sac.

The second negative reason for following Jesus is that I'm not at all sure I could stop if I wanted to. There are quite a few indications in the Bible (have a look at the beginning of the twelfth chapter of Romans) that faith is a gift placed into me, as it were, by God. It becomes a part of what I am, and is only very rarely visible as a discrete entity, rather as the end of my own nose is something I catch sight of only very occasionally. Certainly, the Bible says that some people will abandon their faith, but probably for the same reason that you would end up wanting to abandon your nose if you spent your entire life squinting at it instead of using it naturally and unconsciously in conjunction with the agents of your other senses.

Even on those occasions when I really think I'm seriously on the edge of unbelief or disillusionment, something happens to turn the whole thing upside down. Have you known those moments when, just as you're witnessing some unusually crass piece of behaviour on the part of what's called the Christian church, and you're about to turn away from the whole thing in disgust, you become aware that Jesus himself is watching the same thing over your shoulder and shaking his head as despairingly as you are? It's not easy to trudge dolefully away from an entire faith system when its founder trudges dolefully away beside you.

I heard somewhere of an occasion in one of the Second World War death camps when the suffering Jewish inmates put God on trial for failing them so badly. Eventually a verdict was about to be passed stating that he had not only failed, he did not exist at all. Proceedings had to be abruptly halted at this juncture, however, because it was time for synagogue. Making a decision to stop following Jesus is very much like that. I might decide that I do not possess nasal apparatus, but my decision will not affect the existence of my nose in the slightest.

Perhaps belief and unbelief are two sides of the same coin. You can turn the coin over, but you can't make the side you're not looking at go away. There have been times in my life when I have been extremely grateful for that fact.

Where would I go? How would I stop? I have no answers to those questions.

I follow Jesus because ...
he's so good at judo

'What?'

That was the initial reaction of a friend when I told him the title of this section. 'I may not be the greatest Bible scholar in the world,' he continued, in heavily ironic tones, 'but I feel fairly confident in saying that there's no record in the Gospels of Jesus heaving his enemies over his shoulder, even when the soldiers came for him in the garden. Or have I crassly misinterpreted some vital little passage involving an original Greek word that has a very strong sense of kung fu?'

Well, of course that isn't what I mean. My dictionary tells me that the literal translation of the Japanese word *jujitsu* is 'gentle skill'. One aspect of that gentle skill is the way in which an opponent's weight, speed and aggression can actually be used against him by an expert practitioner. And this is exactly what Jesus was so good at. His gentle skill enabled him to use the weight of other people's prejudices, or anger, or need, or attitudes, or desires, to propel them, often to their surprise and bewilderment, into places where he wanted them to be but they had never expected to find themselves. Some obvious examples spring to mind.

Confronted with the woman taken in adultery, Jesus declined to waste time arguing with the Pharisees and lawyers who had tried to trap him with their question about the woman's punishment under the law. Indeed, his response when it did come was more or less, 'Yes! Yes, of course she must be stoned, that's the law. Get on with it. Get on and stone her. One of you who's never sinned, step up now and throw the first stone.'

Over his shoulder, figuratively speaking, went the lot of 'em. Not a stone was thrown and the woman went away to sort her life out.

That story appears in the Gospel of John, but there are many other examples of divine *jujitsu* throughout all four of the Gospels. Read about Jesus' reply to the chief priests and elders when they questioned his authority in the twentieth chapter of Luke, and enjoy the way he dealt with a question about paying taxes to Caesar in the twenty-second chapter of Matthew. The same gentle skill was employed in many of his parables. The story of the Good Samaritan in the tenth chapter of Luke, for instance, made direct use of his audience's natural sympathies and sheer enjoyment of story to draw them into providing an answer to their own question, 'Who is my neighbour?' As we know, that answer was most certainly not the one they had anticipated.

Later in the New Testament, we find Paul the apostle taking a leaf out of his master's book. Quizzed about Christianity by curious Athenians in the seventeenth chapter of Acts, and faced with a pagan altar inscribed 'To an unknown god', he doesn't squeal, 'New age! New age!' as some of the modern brethren might. Instead he uses the words on that altar as a platform or starting point for his message about the one true God. Paul was quite good at judo as well. — *always?*

It saddens me that, in this age, there remain so few practitioners of this art. It saddens me because people are so much more likely to return to God if they are allowed at least to *begin* the journey on a familiar road. Very few folk make a spiritually positive response simply to being told off, and yet, despite having the example of Jesus in front of us, that's what we very often do. There's a real fear in many Christians that creative interaction with non-Christians is a form of cheating. At best this can result in the sort of bloodless evangelism that won't attract and may well repel.

The other day, for example, an acquaintance named Robert rang to ask if I could offer him some advice. He had been asked to write six spiritually based pieces to be broadcast daily for a week from his local radio station. His producer's brief stated that these Thoughts for the Day should be short, bright and entertaining; they should make at least one good point as clearly as possible, and they should avoid the use of religious language that might be inaccessible to unchurched listeners.

'The thing is,' said Robert, 'I've written them, and I think they're more or less all right, but I wondered if I could drive over and read them to you and get your comments or criticisms. You've done a lot of these things, haven't you?'

I agreed to him coming, but not without trepidation. It was true that I had produced many similar pieces over the years, but I also had wide experience of people urging me to be absolutely frank about the things they had written, and then getting tight-lipped, tearful or just plain cross when I took them at their word.

'You are sure, aren't you,' I said, as I was about to put the phone down, 'that you want me to be perfectly honest?'

'Good heavens, yes!' laughed Robert, as though I was making some sort of silly joke. 'That's why I'm coming, for goodness' sake! What would be the point otherwise?'

As I finally put the phone down, I calmed my fears by reflecting on the fact that Robert was an intelligent, sensitive man who had known a lot of pain in his life. Surely his writing would reflect all those things?

As it turned out, some of them did, but there was one piece that seemed to me lacking in judo skills. 'Can we just look at that last one about the lottery?' I said.

'Right!' Robert nodded.

'Now, in your piece you say this is a very materialistic age, and that, instead of thinking about winning lots of money, people should be thinking about their spiritual lives and realizing how much Jesus has done for them. In fact, you're more or less telling them off for doing the lottery, aren't you?'

'Well, yes, I don't agree with it.'

'But don't you think there could be a more positive route to take than simply saying it's a bad thing – dismissing people's dreams so totally and unsympathetically?'

'Well…'

'Why do people play the lottery?'

'To get rich.'

'Well, that's one way of looking at it. The other way is to say that they yearn for something really wonderful to happen in their lives.'

'Yes, but money isn't—'

'Hold on, hold on! We haven't arrived there yet. They want something wonderful to happen in their lives, something that will change everything. Jesus coming into their lives might be something wonderful that would change everything, right?'

'Right, and that's why—'

'So they've got all the right appetites, but perhaps for the wrong things – do you agree?'

'Well, perhaps, but it's the desire for money that's wrong. I've got to say that.'

'Have you considered, Robert, the fact that, more than once, Jesus offered being rich as a reward for following him?'

Robert stirred uneasily in his chair and shook his head. 'No he didn't. He said it was pretty well impossible for a rich man to get into heaven.'

'What did he say we should store up in heaven?'

'Well – treasure, but he didn't mean money, he was talking about—'

'Hold on, hold on! We haven't got there yet. He was appealing to the part of humanity that wants to be rich, wasn't he? He tells us that it's fine to be rich as long as we've understood what the most important currency of all actually is. Right? And when we get to heaven and we're strolling through the divine shopping precincts, what will that currency be? What will be printed on the wad of heavenly banknotes that angelic bank clerks have issued to us from the account we've built up while we were on earth?'

'Love?'

'Exactly! The currency of heaven is love, and if Jesus comes into our lives we suddenly become heirs to a fortune, and we shall spend it in eternity, and that isn't just playing with words. Maybe we should be saying to the people who do the lottery, "This is great! You have all the right spiritual instincts. You want a real, significant change in your lives and you want to be rich. What you haven't understood is that you can have both those things without paying a pound, and at considerably more favourable odds." What do you think, Robert? Does that make sense as a way to approach that one?'

I looked at him hopefully. He looked back at me like a landlubber cast adrift on a flimsy raft in a bad storm. 'Well – I, er, I think I'd rather leave it as it is, really.'

I was a bit thrown, but then that's judo for you, isn't it?

I follow Jesus because ... he's gentle with people who have been badly hurt

Let me tell you now about one of the most important things that has ever happened to me. I hope it will mean something special to you, and that through it you might understand more about the compassionate heart of God and, much less importantly, a little more about me.

This experience happened in the early hours of the

morning on British Airways flight BA 2028 as it droned through dark European skies from Baku, the capital of Azerbaijan, on its way to Gatwick Airport in England.

I was already feeling quite emotional. Baku was the place where my eldest son, Matthew, was teaching conversational English at a private language school. Sitting on the plane, I was remembering that incredible moment when, on seeing baby Matthew for the first time, I had whispered to myself that this might be the first toy I had ever been given that stood a real chance of not getting broken. Now, just as he was approaching his twenty-fourth birthday, I had spent a week visiting him and exploring a city of intriguing extremes.

Until recently a part of the Soviet Union, Azerbaijan is a Muslim country, shaped – very appropriately considering its geographical position to the east of Turkey – like an eagle flying from west to east. A great oil-producing nation at the turn of the century, it may become so again when the liquid gold begins to flow once more. In the meantime, the Soviets seem to have sucked the country dry and departed, leaving a people who have perhaps lost the will, the way and the means to achieve a reasonable standard of living. On every road and in every street I saw stalls selling either cheap plastic goods, spare parts for cars which suffer from the appallingly bad roads, or shoe-mending services, essential because of the equally uneven and unrepaired pavements. On several occasions I came across elderly folk sitting resignedly beside old, dusty domestic weighing machines, presumably hoping that odd passers-by might feel a sudden uncontrollable urge to pay for the privilege of knowing their weight. Some roadside stalls, often but by no means invariably presided over by children, were nothing more than cardboard boxes on which stood two or three bottles of fizzy orange drink of uncertain age. The streets were filled with taxis, mainly Russian-produced Ladas, in such profusion that it was difficult to see who the potential customers might be, other than fellow taxi-drivers whose vehicles had broken down. It had all been rather depressing.

On the other hand, some aspects of Azerbaijani culture were enviable. I came across small children walking home together in the dark with no apparent fear of attack, and all the women I spoke to had that same sense of being safe in most of the streets at any time of day or night. There is no unemployment benefit in Azerbaijan, and the old-age pension is only five pounds per month, but elderly people are not neglected, abandoned or benignly disposed of. They have a place in their families until death. I found the Azerbaijani people warmly hospitable and more than willing to share the little that they had.

Matthew's apartment, shared with two other teachers, was on the second floor of what must once have been a very palatial private residence. Baku was full of these reminders of a bygone age, splendidly ornate buldings that have been allowed to decay and crumble to the extent that the filthy stairwells and back yards resembled the set of *Oliver*, or those old photographs you sometimes see of poverty-stricken areas of Victorian London. I gathered that there was quite a problem with rats in Baku.

I stayed with Matthew for just under a week, greatly enjoying his company as always, and taking a particular pleasure in the experience of seeing him function so well in such a different context. Some aspects of my eldest son's childhood, especially the period when I was ill more than a decade ago, were far from easy for him, so it was good to see the present beginning to eclipse the past. It was hard to leave Matthew when my stay ended, but not at all hard to leave Baku Airport, which must be one of the most depressing places on earth, highly reminiscent as it was of a very low-budget set from the old television series *The Avengers.*

As I sat on the plane, bracing myself for a journey that would last for more than five hours, I thought about the people of Azerbaijan and about Matthew, about the rest of my family, with whom I would soon be reunited, and about the various challenges that awaited me at home. I found myself gradually slipping into an all too familiar mood of self-doubt and despair. There are times, and this point of transition was one of them, when faith and hope mean nothing, and all my reference points and benchmarks seem to become insubstantial and float away beyond my grasp. Some of you will know what I mean when I say that I almost shuddered with the complexity and puzzlement of simply being alive, and with a deep dread of something in the recesses of my mind that I could not (or would not) name for fear of acknowledging its existence.

Oddly enough, these alarming moments have quite often been the prelude to learning something important from God, perhaps because it's easier to fill an empty vessel than a full one – I don't really know. On this occasion, though, there was no immediate sign of such a lesson, because things started to look up.

It's amazing and faintly depressing, isn't it, to note how the arrival of a meal and a small bottle of wine can temporarily disperse such dark fancies, and I was greatly pleased, in addition, to learn that the in-flight entertainment was to be *Good Will Hunting*, a film which had featured heavily in the Oscar award ceremony for that year. I had really wanted to see that film. Now I was going to. When the video began to play I clamped my headphones to my ears with both hands to cut out extraneous noise, and settled down to enjoy a solid hour or two of entertainment.

Good Will Hunting is about Will, a young man who, although gifted to the point of genius in the area of mathematics, is severely handicapped in his practical personal and social interactions because of traumatic experiences as a child. The first light of salvation comes through his encounter with an unconventional therapist, played by Robin Williams, who, after a series of sessions in which his patient becomes increasingly accessible, offers him a file containing details of his troubled past and says simply, 'It's not your fault.' The young man retreats, unable to handle such a proposition, but the therapist persists until, after the fourth or fifth repetition of this phrase, Will breaks down for the first time and weeps on his therapist's shoulder.

I wept as well. Buckets. Quite embarrassing really.

Who did I weep for?

Well, for a start I wept for the children in care I once worked with. I had been through the same process with many of them, saying as clearly as I could, 'Some things are undoubtedly your fault, and you must take responsibility for them, but these things, the things over which you had no control, the things which create a whirlwind of fear and anger and guilt in you whenever they rise to the surface of your mind – these are not your fault, and they never were. The time has come to accept that and move on.' Sometimes I had even gone through their files with them at bedtime, especially when they were just about to be fostered or adopted. It was a revelation to many of them. At such times I was privileged to witness a lot of bravery and tears.

I wept for Matthew, always deeply loved and cared for, but nevertheless with very real demons of his own to exorcise, demons whose presence is certainly not his fault, and I wished I could go back to help him do it, even though he appears to be managing very well on his own.

I wept a little for the people of Azerbaijan, seemingly always being used or abused by someone or other, and especially for the children, who are living through bewildering changes in the historical and political ethos of their country, reckoned to be the third most corrupt in the world. They have so little at the moment, and that lack, and the confusion many must feel, is not their fault.

I even wept a little for myself, and for the rest of my family when their lives are unfairly darkened by the indefinable shadow that has oppressed me since childhood.

Finally, and this is important to me because I believe God wants me to pass it on wherever I go, I wept for so many members of the Christian church who have been taught only about the anger and retribution and inflexibility of God. I wept for all the men, women and children who have never really understood that Jesus, the Lord of creation, who justly demands full repentance from all those who wish to come home to the Father, looks with deep compassion on those who struggle to live with wounds from long ago. Laying a hand gently on their shoulder, he says, 'I know what they did to you, I know how they hurt you and made you feel guilty and worthless. I know how, over and over again, the past rises in your throat to snatch away the very breath of life, and I also know that it's not your fault. Please hear me say those words to you once more – it's not your fault.'

I follow Jesus because ...
you're allowed to even if you're useless with practical problems, general technology, and especially computers

I have nothing but admiration and deep regard for those who are practically and technologically inclined. Good for them, I say. More power to their elbows or fingertips or whatever. It's just that the technological revolution seems to have passed me by, and I'm so glad prayer isn't conducted through the Internet. I have, it's true, just about mastered my computer enough to write on it (that's what I'm doing in a rather laboured fashion at this very moment), but it's so much cleverer than I am. Don't you just hate that message that appears on the screen after you've written something, saying, 'DO YOU REALLY WANT TO SAVE *THIS*?'

I'm similarly intimidated by the cashpoint machine next to one of the banks in our local town of Hailsham. After asking you to enter your personal identification number and the amount of money you want to draw out, the final question is, 'WITH OR WITHOUT ADVICE?' In this context, the word 'advice' presumably means 'information' or 'receipt', but I always opt for 'WITHOUT ADVICE', for fear that the machine might produce a slip of paper saying,

> Doesn't it occur to you that you're going through your money at a rather alarming rate? You've asked for £50, but if I were you, I'd take £30. You know as well as I do that if you've got it in your pocket, you'll spend it, and you've got a lot of things coming up next month. Just for once, do think! Money doesn't grow on trees, you know...

I really am defeated by most practical tasks (I've only just understood that WD40 is not a postcode), all machinery and every aspect of technology. A while ago, for instance, I purchased one of those items that purports to be a telephone, fax and answering machine all in one. My naive hope was that this incredible invention would make life much easier. After all, in theory it should have done, shouldn't it? I'm in need of all three of those functions on a regular basis. The blurb on the side of the box seemed to promise that my new toy would do just about everything except cook bacon and eggs for me before I started work in the morning. Encouragingly, it was accompanied by one of those user-friendly manuals that are supposed to allow the most thickheaded dumbo to programme his or her new purchase successfully for daily use.

Well, yes, but what the authors of this idiot-proof publication with the section headings in big black print and little cartoon figures pointing smilingly to things failed to realize is that I have taken ordinary, old-fashioned idiocy to new and giddy heights. Like the writers of just about every other easy-to-follow set of instructions that I've ever read, these well-meaning people had a tendency to make sudden, wild jumps between one stepping stone and an impossibly distant other, leaving me to flounder helplessly out of my depth in between.

One day I'm going to write a special instruction book for all the hollow-brains like me – if my computer is good enough to allow me to, that is. I can promise you that it won't just be user friendly, it will be user *intimate*. There will be chapters on such subjects as how to boil an egg, how to change a plug and how to put up a shelf that will actually hold things. These sets of instructions will take readers gently by their trembling, inexpert hands and lead them like little children into new worlds of confidence and achievement. The section about changing one of the wheels on your car, for instance, will begin in the following way:

1 Have a cup of tea (see Chapter One – 'Making Tea').
2 Read the paper.
3 Have another cup of tea.
4 Give up the idea of changing the wheel.

5 Decide you might as well do it in a minute, as you have nothing better to do.

6 Have another cup of tea.

7 Stroll outside and stand in front of your car (in the about-to-be-run-over-but-don't-care position). Behave in a casual fashion. If the car gets the slightest inkling that you're planning to do something to it, it will turn awkward and sulk.

8 Now, the first tricky bit. Do you see those four big round things, one at each corner of the car? Those are the wheels. One of them isn't working properly because the rubber thing called a tyre that runs round the outside hasn't got any air in it. We're going to take that whole wheel off and put a different one in its place. Do you believe in your heart that such a thing could be possible?

9 Go back in and have another cup of tea, revise what you've learned so far, then we'll go back outside and I'll explain how to work out which wheel is the one that needs to be replaced...

Long before this point is reached in normal instruction manuals, technologically challenged folk like me will have been instructed to 'invert the lateral flange in relation to the inward angle of the outer rim', or some other such meaningless command. Ignorant of the nature or location of either flanges or outer rims, we will have given up and gone in to have a cup of tea and read the newspaper. I think my instruction book will sell like hot cakes, don't you? Come to think of it, I might include a chapter on making cakes. First, locate the kitchen...

Anyway, the results of my attempt to get the phone/fax/answering machine operating properly were disappointing to say the least. Friends who called for a little chat were instructed by a chillingly sepulchral voice to press something they hadn't got in order to initiate a procedure that they hadn't heard of; people who tried to fax documents were asked to leave messages after a 'long tone' which never actually materialized in any case; and those who attempted to leave messages found themselves verbally assaulted by a series of pre-recorded Dalek-like messages informing them, among other things, that they had performed an illegal action and were liable to prosecution. An expert, called by me from the public telephone box down the road, investigated the whole situation and detected a serious fault in my system almost immediately. Me. It was being operated by an idiot.

I've never got on with all these space-age watches either. Frustratedly trying to poke minuscule buttons in the right, impossibly complex permutation with a blunt pencil in poor light when you've mislaid your spectacles strikes me as an overrated pastime. I've tried and failed a number of times. If you were to sit in the confusion of my study for a while, you would hear abandoned digital watches intermittently peeping out obsolete or wrongly-adjusted reminders from hidden places, like little electronic frogs in a swamp of folders and box files and unanswered letters. I never see them, and I shall certainly never understand them, but I have to confess that I do take a quiet pleasure in their company, particularly in the morning. The dawn chorus of the lost digitals has become part of my life.

My daughter is quick with modern stuff, which is just as well, but one day, when she was about 10, she produced an ordinary cardboard box and asked if we could make a carriage for Honey, our foster-hamster. The gods of chaos relish my efforts with glue and scissors and cardboard. Katy and I share a staggering lack of talent in this area, but we love getting into a complete mess together as we feverishly try to *make* something. Isambard Kingdom Brunel may have been proud of his completed Clifton Suspension Bridge (go and see it if you're ever in that part of Bristol), but no more so than Katy and I were of our sticky, unstable, rickety collection of toilet-roll holders and bits of cereal packet. *We* had *made* it together. Honey managed to mime her intention of leaving home if we made her get in it, and I don't blame her, but it just about rolled along, and we thought it was wonderful.

So why did God not choose this age of superior technology for the visit of his son? Most people are not like me when it comes to these things. Surely, twentieth-century global communication systems would have been far more preferable than painstakingly passing on the message from person to person? Apparently not. But *why* not? Presumably because Christianity always was *about* person-to-person communication. It always was about individuals being special. More people come to the Christian faith through one-to-one contact than in any other way. It had to start like that. And, despite the worst efforts of some who call themselves Christians, Christianity survives. Unstable, rickety, homemade and in continual need of repair it may be, but it still rolls along – and, as the body of Jesus on earth, we have made it together.

I follow Jesus because ...
he's interested in the heart of worship
rather than the form

I know as much about worship as the Pope knows about sharing toothpaste or hot-water bottles, but it has long been the case in Christian circles that specialized knowledge is regarded as a sort of public well. Anyone is entitled to go and draw a bucketful for distribution to others who aren't sure where the well is, or can't be bothered to go for themselves. That's why very married people are asked to do seminars on being single, and whimsical poets end up lecturing on practical Christianity. Do you think I'm joking? If only I was.

Having made this very defensive point, however, I must confess that I have both enjoyed and suffered an enormous amount of worship of many different kinds during my travels over the last few years. If you will allow me to cast a retrospective eye over some of these experiences, we may discover something about the way in which God regards these various expressions. (I only said 'may'.)

There are no fixed rules about the quality of worship, are there? Bad worship (like good worship) can be formal or informal, musical or unmusical, modern or traditional, long or short, prepared or impromptu. No doubt some or all of these are very important considerations, but they are not the criteria that, as far as I can see, bring joy or sorrow to the business of paying homage to God, which is what I understand worship to be. Let me tell you about two very negative experiences, and two very positive ones. (Forgive me – I'm hopelessly anecdotal.)

The first negative one occurred in a church in the north of England that, as a matter of interest (nothing to do with me, I hope) no longer exists. There were about 200 people present on this bright Sunday morning, and it must have been one of the best organized services I've ever attended. The notices were discreet, the prayers were beautifully worded and read by voices warm with sincerity, the Scripture readings were delivered with emphasis and feeling, and the music – oh, the music! You should have heard the music during the actual worship session. It rose and fell and ebbed and flowed and linked and joined and boomed and hushed like well-oiled, complex machinery, guided by a worship leader who conducted the congregation and, as far as one could tell, the members of the Trinity themselves, as though they were some great spiritual orchestra. At last, as we approached the time when I was due to speak, this same worship leader extended his hand dramatically towards me and, when the final chorus had sunk like a dying ballerina to its close, said in a voice that throbbed and resonated with feeling, 'Now, Adrian, will you come and speak to us?'

And I said, 'No.'

I wasn't just trying to muck up their wonderful event – I did get up and speak after that, of course – but the thing was that I'd hated that service. It felt terribly unreal and contrived, and I wanted to break the spell if it wasn't one cast by the Holy Spirit. Later, I learned that the church was suffering a great corporate hurt, and I realized that the 'perfect' service was nothing more than a huge piece of sticking plaster.

The second negative experience was almost an opposite to the one I've just told you about. In this case almost no preparations had been made for an event that had been in my diary for over a year. When I arrived there was much talk about 'letting the Holy Spirit take charge of events'. Well, all I can say is that if the Holy Spirit was in charge, he shouldn't have been because he didn't do a very good job. No one seemed to know quite what was supposed to happen next at any given point, and when the praise session arrived it threatened never to go away again. Those musicians and singers got completely carried away and gave us a real foretaste of eternity. An exaggeration, of course – it only lasted about three days.

Positive experiences? I suppose the one that stands out is an Easter Day service in Norwich Cathedral. The hymns were traditional, the spoken words were pure prayer-book, and the address was worthy without being inspired, but there are sometimes great benefits to be had from the democracy of a fixed liturgy. As the bright April sun streamed in through the windows that morning, my heart soared in worship. I wanted to fly up to the roof of that beautiful building and shout out my appreciation of the risen, living Jesus. It was wonderful.

Then there was that Pentecostal service in a kind of glorified shed in a depressed area of one of our large cities. The people gathered in this place were more like a bus queue than a congregation. I would guess that most of them were pretty hard up, and I'm quite sure that, in the view of many of my theologically expert brethren, some of them would be considered seriously 'off the ball', if you'll forgive the expression. But there was so much love there – such a sense of Jesus being present. And when the poorly played, cheap guitars and the squeaky violin got going, I found the tears coming to my eyes. We really worshipped.

What made these two services so much more relevant and meaningful to me than the two disasters I mentioned previously? Why did the worship touch my heart and spirit in such widely varying situations? I would suggest that the answer is something to do with reality, and something to do with what, for want of a better word, we might call 'heart'.

Reality demands that we allow for situations and people to be as they are when we come together to acknowledge God, recognizing and giving permission for pain and joy to rise with exactly equal validity to the heavenly throne when we give ourselves in worship. How many times have you heard worship leaders exhorting folk to leave their troubles aside for an hour and make a sacrifice of praise? That's not what it means, for goodness' sake! We don't leave our troubles aside. On the contrary, we collect up the baggage that's weighing us down so uncomfortably and carry it to God. That's the sacrifice – that we go anyway, and we say, 'Despite this weight, which I can't yet put down, despite this pain which fills me right now, I will worship you.' Check it out in the Psalms.

Heart is much more difficult to define, but wherever there is warmth, humour, goodwill, the glow of genuine kindness and a readiness in key people to abandon their personal agendas when necessary, worship will come alive, because Jesus inhabits all of those things, whether they occur in a cathedral or a shed. I wouldn't give you twopence for streamlined worship that has no heart.

Reality and heart – that's what I reckon. Within reasonable limits I would say that anything, anyone, anywhere, any music, any words can be relevant as long as those two little items are on the corporate agenda. Rather unsurprisingly, if you amalgamate ultimate reality with pure heart, you'll find Jesus, and if he's not there it's not worth bothering anyway.

In fact, of course, true worship is much broader than a few choruses, or an hour together on a Sunday. It's about giving all that we are and all that we do to God. The challenge is actually much greater than we think, but don't worry – as with everything else in the Christian life, Jesus has made it quite clear that failure is not only anticipated, but catered for as well.

I follow Jesus because … now and then I get the chance to follow his example and stir people up

The best two examples of this that I know, as far as my own work is concerned, are the following. The first, an imagined account of a meeting in my home, has previously only appeared on the Internet, where it attracted wide and wildly varying responses. I was glad, because that was exactly what it was supposed to do. What do you think?

Example 1

I'm taking advantage of a half-hour break to tell you about some of the people who are gathered in my sitting room at this very moment. Most of them represent oppressed Christian minorities, suffering brothers and sisters of yours and mine who have been dealt with very roughly by the wider church, and I just know that your hearts will go out to them in love and sympathy. I cannot be away for too lengthy a period, as some of these minority representatives are likely to exercise their proclivities rather indiscriminately on each other, if you see what I mean.

You don't see what I mean? Ah, well, let me explain.

Sitting side by side on the floor by the piano, for instance, are Phil and Bob, who run a helpline for those who see disembowelling as a natural and essential part of any intimate relationship. Some of us were in tears just now as we heard about the crass way in which these two fine young men were more or less rejected by their local church when they dared to suggest that the forcible removal of internal organs should become a regular feature of Sunday worship.

'The thing is,' said Bob, 'a lot of people have got a very blinkered and old-fashioned idea of what disembowelling is all about. We're not into rushing wildly around with knives from morning to night, are we, Phil?'

As we all laughed at this absurd caricature, Phil's good-natured face broke into an infectious grin. 'Good heavens, no,' he chuckled, 'we're not monsters, you know. We just think that if the need to disembowel and be disembowelled is part of the way we've been created, then there should be some recognition of that by the body of the church, and an opportunity on Sundays to express ourselves at least as openly as everyone else.'

At this point a member of the group rather insensitively put forward a suggestion that disembowelling was a grotesque and appalling practice that invariably resulted in a lengthy and agonizing death, and might therefore be outside the will of God. It was good to see how patiently Bob and Phil handled this, but the pain in their eyes told its own story of similar hurts in the past, and our hearts went out to them – metaphorically.

'Look,' said Bob, 'we're the same as everyone else, right? We go to work, go to the supermarket, watch television – all the things that ordinary people do. The only real difference is that in order for us to feel fulfilled on the deepest level we like to cut open abdominal cavities and drag out the contents. It really is as simple as that, and if anyone can find anywhere in the New Testament where Jesus in any way specifically condemns that kind of behaviour, well, I'd just like them to show me where it is.'

'And if *he* doesn't condemn it,' added Phil quietly, 'it's hard to see why anyone else should.'

Something in the calm dignity of these responses precluded further comment or criticism, and our attention turned to a reserved but pleasant-looking lady called June, who had been listening interestedly from a stool on the other side of the room.

'It's really encouraged me to hear what Phil and Bob are saying,' she began shyly, 'because I've been trying to introduce human sacrifice as a regular activity at church weekends, and so far I've met nothing but opposition from the leadership.'

'What exactly *is* their problem?' asked someone wonderingly.

June spread her arms wide and shook her head. 'That's exactly what I'd like to know!' she exclaimed. 'Apart from the personal outlet that it provides for me, I've tried to point out again and again what a good group activity it would be for people who don't always know each other very well.' June's eyes shone with the bright light of the enthusiast as she warmed to her subject. 'You break up into groups, you see, and each group has a different job. One lot gets sent off to collect dry paper and firewood, another sorts out a good strong stake and some rope and matches and that sort of thing, and the rest do sausages on sticks, and jugs of squash and sandwiches and whatnot, to have round the pyre when it really gets going.'

This happy picture of bright and busy mutual involvement was greeted by expressions of interest and nods of approval from most of us, but the same troubled person who had already carped at disembowelling seemed to feel it necessary to throw cold water over this idea as well.

'How do you choose which person is going to be sacrificed?'

This was met by little gasps and sighs of incredulity and a general shaking of heads from the rest of us, but we needn't have worried. June held her ground well.

'Nobody who doesn't actually want to be burnt alive should have any pressure put on them,' she declared firmly. 'That would be totally wrong, and, in my view, quite unnecessary. Church people do tend to be a little wary about trying out new things, as we all know, but I think once they'd understood what it was all about there'd be no lack of volunteers. I sometimes can't believe,' added June, her eyes suddenly filled with unshed tears, 'that people like Phil and Bob and me, whose only crime is to look for fulfilment through things like disembowelling and human sacrifice, are *so* marginalized by the church. Why are people so *frightened* by the needs of others?'

We all sat in silence for a moment, filled with unspoken sympathy as we pondered this seemingly unanswerable question. The silence was broken eventually by an elderly lady dressed in a rubber suit and carrying a spiked metal ball on the end of a chain.

'I suppose,' she said tentatively, 'that something like sado-masochism, which in itself is obviously morally neutral, tends to be given a bad name by a small number of irresponsible people who use it for their own selfish ends.' She sighed deeply, gazing into the distance as she went on. 'In the old days, you know, it was so different. We used to have our own rack at home when father was alive, and on special occasions we'd pull it out and put an aunt on it – it was usually an aunt, I seem to remember – and, you know, we'd all have a turn at the handle. It was *such* fun. A much greater sense of the extended family.' She giggled at her own little joke. 'Nowadays, if you bring, say, a thumbscrew into a prayer meeting everyone backs away and gets all sniffy. Church, generally, was so much better in the old days in every way. The traditional hymns were lovely, and we didn't get all muddled up, confusing what we believed with the way we lived.'

After that the floodgates were opened. A small, round, balding man who had said nothing until now, sliced the air with scything gestures as he described a lifetime of survival at church in the face of outright disapproval of his deeply felt decapitational needs. Asked if he had ever found a partner, the little man held his head in both hands and shook it miserably from side to side. Most congregations are a long way from regarding mutual decapitation beween consenting adults as an acceptable norm.

So much unhappiness! An athletic-looking young lady painted a vivid picture for us of what it meant to battle the widespread taboo against jumping out at people in dark, lonely places with a chainsaw, a middle-aged banker talked with pride of the stable, monogamous relationship that he has enjoyed for 20 years with a fellow arsonist, and we heard from a small group of professional men and women who are in the process of establishing an information and exchange service for those who describe their future lives as 'meaningless without access to napalm' – all folk whom the church has heartlessly rejected for the flimsiest of reasons.

I must go back to them now, but I do ask you to consider the fact that these poor folk are as much a part of the church as you and I. We've come such a long way in broadening our attitudes. Let's not stop now. Thank goodness we live in such increasingly enlightened times! Do you not agree that the spirit of tolerance abroad in the church at present indicates a strong chance that the so-called peculiarities of these persecuted ones will very soon become a normal part of everyday church life?

And isn't that what we all want?

Example 2

The second example appeared in a newspaper published in Holland, a country where the issues involved are particularly relevant ones, and it began with the following question.

Who is more dangerous to society, a murderer or a liberal professor of theology?

Forgive me for asking a question that is so easy to answer. It's just that I sometimes get confused about issues that other people seem to find very straightforward and simple to resolve. I suppose this particular question may have been complicated for me by the strange thing that happened as I was trying to work out our income tax on my computer the other day. What happened was this. Just as everything was beginning to make financial sense, the list of figures on my screen faded away, to be replaced by something that, at first, I took to be an extract from a film.

The scene before me was a superb baronial hall furnished and decorated in a style combining extravagance and good taste in such a startlingly attractive manner, that I felt a wild yearning to be able to leap through the screen of the monitor and enter that place myself. At both sides of a long, highly polished table running the length of the room, were seated cloaked figures who seemed somehow too serene and ethereally statuesque to be truly human. Sitting at the end of the table farthest from me sat a magnificent man with a huge beard and impossibly deep eyes. He was of the same type and quality as the others around the table, but more so, if you understand my meaning.

Happening to glance at the very top edge of my screen, I suddenly noticed that the legend {HEAVEN – FUTURE VISION. WPS} was visible in the place where the filename usually appears. So that was it! This was no film extract. For some reason I was in the privileged position of actually witnessing an event which was yet to happen in the heavenly realms, an event which must be linked to earthly matters, I surmised, since there is, of course, neither present, future nor past in heaven. And those creatures around the table – they must be angels! Yes, now that I studied them more closely I could clearly see the significantly large protrusions beneath their cloaks, just at the point where the shoulder blades would normally be located. As for the grand personage at the end of the table – well, who could he be but God himself?

And this gathering – was it possible that I could be witnessing a meeting of the committee for divine admissions?

Excited beyond words, I watched and listened as a bright-faced servant holding a large bunch of golden keys in one hand, a notebook in the other, and with a heavy book clenched under his arm, ran in through a door at the end of the hall without knocking and, standing at the head of the table, spoke with an intriguing blend of familiarity and respect to the creator of the universe.

'There's a man just turned up unexpectedly at the gate,' he said, 'who would like to come in. What shall I do?'

'Name?' enquired God interestedly.

The servant glanced at his pad.

'Er, Kuitert,' he replied, 'Harry Kuitert.'

God frowned and thought for a moment, then shook his head slowly from side to side.

'Never heard of him,' he said. He turned to the angel on his right. 'Mean anything to you, Gabriel?'

'Can't place him at all. What was the name again?'

'Harry Kuitert,' enunciated the servant slowly and clearly. 'Sounds vaguely Dutch to me.'

'Oh, dear!' muttered an angel near the bottom of the table.

'No,' pronounced Gabriel after staring into the distance for a moment, 'sorry, drawn a complete blank there.'

'What shall I tell him then?' enquired the servant.

'Well, tell him he doesn't exist,' said God. 'Tell him he only thinks he exists, but he's made a mistake. Easily done.'

The servant referred to his notebook again.

'He said some other things. Claims he was a professor of theology on earth, and—'

'Of course, that in itself doesn't necessarily rule him out of heaven,' interrupted God genially.

'And he says he wrote books questioning your omniscience and omnipotence.'

'Well, he's probably right,' chuckled God, 'because however hard I try I can't make myself remember anyone called

Kuitert. That may be a source of satisfaction to him once he's got over the fact that he doesn't exist.'

'Well, he did give me this to show you as well,' said the servant, taking the heavy book from under his arm and placing it on the end of the table. 'He says he wrote it, and I've just had a quick read of it.' He thumbed his way through until he came to a specific page. 'There's a bit here about how Jesus' followers deliberately exaggerated his importance, and about how Jesus himself can't possibly have thought he was God.'

'Well, there you are, then,' said God, leaning back and smacking the table with an air of finality, 'he can't possibly exist. No one who's seriously interested in getting into heaven could possibly have taught dangerous rubbish like that. Why, that would be blasphemy! In any case, some old book doesn't prove a thing. This bloke's friends could have written it – made it all up. No, Harry Kuitert is a figment of his own imagination.'

'He did also say when he, er, thought he was alive,' persisted the servant deferentially, 'that he regretted robbing people of their trusted image of Jesus, someone they could speak to and trust and get close to and all that, but he had to do it to be honest to himself. Awfully strong on that, he was. Very clever man, he seems – I mean – he would seem, if he existed.'

'Oh, he seems clever, does he?'

The expression on God's face as he suddenly levered himself to his feet at this point was really quite frightening. He pointed towards the door and addressed the servant in ringing tones.

'You go and tell him that if one single person fails to come through that gate because Harry Kuitert was *clever* enough to know that they didn't need saving from an eternity of missing out on being here with us, he will spend the same amount of time wishing that we were right about him not existing. And for goodness' sake send in someone who really is clever enough to know me, a five-year-old would do, or one of my mentally handicapped friends...'

Just then the scene faded, and my tax calculations reappeared on the screen. That's what happened, and that's why, for a little while, I was confused about the answer to that question I asked earlier on. Silly, wasn't it?

Who is more dangerous to society, a murderer or a liberal professor of theology?

As if there was any doubt!

I follow Jesus because ...
he's the only one who knows the path to genuinely solid ground

You've heard of Tunbridge Wells, haven't you? It's famous as a symbol of conservatism, spelt with both a small and a large 'c', and is popularly supposed to be the home of a character who writes frequent, angry letters to *The Times* newspaper, signing them 'Disgusted of Tunbridge Wells'. Visually it's a rather beautiful place, with fine Georgian and Victorian buildings nestling in a valley at the foot of a magnificent piece of common land that's as relaxing to stroll in today as it must have been 200 years ago.

Now, before you begin to suspect that this section has been sponsored by the Tunbridge Wells Tourist Board, let me tell you something else about this charming collection of giant dolls' houses standing on the border between the counties of Kent and Sussex. I grew up there. This is not a fact that features heavily in the town's publicity material – in fact, it doesn't feature in it at all – but the 18 years I spent there were very significant ones for me. I roamed restlessly through the streets of Tunbridge Wells for hour after hour and day after day throughout the whole of my teenage period, searching for something or nothing or someone or no one. It was a depressing time, but it also had a sort of rotten richness, like leaf mould. I was quite relieved when I left. I had begun to think that this dismal decaying process was irreversible, and that I would never get away from the place or the negative image of myself that clung to it.

About 18 months ago I discovered in myself a need to be there again. Why? I was able to identify two reasons.

First, we were seriously on the verge of moving house. For 16 years we had lived in a three-storey Victorian house in East Sussex. We moved there when Matthew, our eldest child, was nine years old, and Joe, the next one down, was nearly four. It was the house in which our children grew up and it saw deep sorrows, great joys and an awful lot of ordinary day-to-day living. It was a house with many rooms, but not a great deal of space, except in the kitchen, which we knew we would miss very much, as my wife and I and most of our friends have been kitchen-dwellers all our lives. The house we were moving to was larger and closer to the countryside, and for those reasons we looked forward to the change. Bridget and I are fairly nomadic by inclination, and neither of us usually minds upheaval.

I found, though, that an unexpectedly dark place threatened to open up beneath me as a result of this plan for change in our lives. It was as though the ground was trembling very slightly under my feet, creating a quite irrational fear that some unidentifiable abyss was about to appear and swallow me. Every now and then, pictures of the streets I had known so very well in Tunbridge Wells flashed into my mind and I wanted to be there, unhappy, but in control.

The other identifiable reason for this desire to return seemed to be the fact of my mother's death in December the previous year. On a not very accessible level I felt my grown-up orphaning very deeply as the anniversary of her death drew closer, and the inner drive to be near to where she had been was strong.

Of course, I was wrapped round by the security blanket of my own immediate family, and that was why I knew I would not actually be endlessly roaming the streets of Tunbridge Wells for the next few months. But that tremor made me think.

What *was* my solid ground?

I wrote somewhere that the resurrection of Jesus redefined solid ground, and that once you have accepted that redefinition, there is a shakiness about any other support system than the one which upholds and protects the part of you that will one day live with him. I continue to believe that with all my heart, but I am aware that, every now and then, I still cling nervously to rocks that look solid, but are bound to sink into the sand when I put my full weight on them. Let us pray for ourselves and each other as we learn how to find our safety truly in Jesus.

Oh, and please don't be put off visiting Tunbridge Wells, by the way. It's a beautiful town.

I follow Jesus because ...
he defends us and battles for us, and has been through a terrible storm for us

Do you like thunderstorms? I love them. The last major one in our part of the world was awesome and Armageddon-like, the mother and father of all thunderstorms. I had never heard such a volume of natural sound in my life before. It was as though some cosmic giant had tried to carry too many planets at once and ended up bouncing six or seven of them down the stairs of his giant mansion. The very air shook.

When such cataclysmic explosions vibrate the very foundations of the house in which we cower, and lightning splits the night sky into jagged fissures of blinding light, it really is very hard not to believe that God is trying to say something significant about someone or other. As I say, I love violent storms usually, but on this occasion, almost without thinking, I found myself reviewing the last week or two, just to check that I hadn't committed a sin worthy of such a dramatic response. Silly, isn't it, but there we are. I am silly sometimes.

The other thing that occurred to me was that when movie-makers like Steven Spielberg witness phenomena like this, they must itch to get their rich, ingenious fingers on the control buttons of such wildly spectacular effects. It's rather pleasant to know, isn't it, that all the wealth and persuasive power of Hollywood put together would never offer sufficient incentive to God to sell off his 'storm rights'.

The next day a friend called Helga rang to talk about two things. First of all she wanted to talk about the storm. Hadn't it been amazing? Yes, it had. Wasn't the thunder loud? Goodness, yes, louder than any thunder any of us had ever heard before! Wasn't it extraordinary how, every now and then, the lightning suddenly lit up every detail of the surrounding countryside in such a vivid way? It certainly was. A bit scary, eh? Well, yes, perhaps just a little…

We enjoyed a good mutual chill and thrill about the storm, and then Helga started to talk about something that, at first, seemed quite unrelated to that subject.

'Did you know,' she asked, 'that I've got a young girl of about 18 or 19 living in the house next door to me?'

'Yes,' I replied, 'one of my sons knows her a bit. She's called Wendy, isn't she?'

'That's right,' said Helga, 'and she's a nice girl really, a bit all over the place, but then she's only young and she's living on her own. Anyway, this morning there was this bunch of neighbours discussing something very sort of intensely not far from my front door when I got back from shopping, and when they saw me they called me over. They were talking about Wendy – well, more moaning than talking really, and they seemed to be enjoying every minute of it. I asked what exactly she was supposed to have done, and everyone started rabbiting on all at once about the noise she makes when she gets in late at night. "But she's not always late," I said, "and anyway, she's only 18. We can't expect her to behave like a nun just because we all like going to bed at 10 o'clock in the evening, can we?"

'This didn't go down too well with the lynch mob, as you've probably guessed, and there were more than a few glares in my direction, but they were obviously determined to get me on their side one way or the other, so then they produced their secret weapon. "Tell her," one of them commanded the person next to her, "what you saw during the storm last night." Well, then this sort of low hum of scandalized agreement rose from the rest of the bunch, and the commanded one gathered herself together all dramatically and spoke in low, carefully enunciated tones. "If you look out of my bedroom window you can see Wendy's back garden. And right at the height of the storm, when the thunder was crashing and the lightning was flashing, I happened to look out of my window, and there on her lawn I saw – well, I saw a young man doing somersaults on the grass in his underpants – in a thunderstorm, would you believe?"

'The lynch mob moved back half an inch at this so they could study my face for signs that this evidence of blatant evil had finally brought me round to their way of thinking. I looked at them for a moment, this little bunch of grim-lipped, respectable people, and I said, "Well, that seems quite a reasonable thing to do during a thunderstorm, if you ask me. Next time one happens I might go out and do the same thing. Although," I added to the lady who had told the story, "I don't suppose you'll be quite as keen to watch when it's me doing somersaults, will you?"

'I went through my front door leaving the lynch mob silent with their mouths hanging open, but I don't think they can have stayed quiet for long, do you? I'm afraid Wendy and I are both going to be in the firing line from now on.'

After my conversation with Helga had ended I sat by the telephone for some time, thinking about that young man rolling around on the grass in his underwear, celebrating his sheer excitement at witnessing the way in which the world performed its very own *son et lumière*. G. K. Chesterton, author of the Father Brown stories, and perhaps my favourite author of all time, would have so appreciated the fact that someone was doing something that felt entirely appropriate to those abnormal circumstances, even though that something seemed bizarre and excessive to others who dared not step beyond the bounds of what is expected.

I thought about Helga and felt glad that someone had been strong enough to resist joining in with the hymn of hate and disapproval that had obviously been getting nicely into tune when she first arrived on the scene.

And I thought about that little bunch of people who had discovered some unity in their common dislike for the way in which another person behaved. 'Ah,' they would want to say to me, 'but what about the underpants? What are the implications of the underpants? What do you have to say about that?' Well, I have nothing to say about that. It's none of my business. But whatever those sinister implications may be, they can't be much worse than ganging up on a young girl behind her back, when she probably needs real, warm, constructive support from her immediate community.

Finally, I thought about God, and the way in which he must yearn for those of us who call ourselves Christians to be aware of the great storms of spiritual warfare that roll and crash around the unseen but crucial battlegrounds of creation. I thought about how much he would like to see us throwing off the stifling garments of meaningless religion so that we may vulnerably, wildly celebrate in the sight of others, the fact that however much thunder and lightning may be flung around the universe, the battle is won by the Lord, and has been ever since a young man called Jesus, dressed only in a loincloth, cried out in a loud voice, 'It is finished!'

I follow Jesus because ...
he does miracles

I'm enormously comforted by the resurrection. It is, of course, the greatest miracle of all as far as we humans are concerned, a shining and ever-present promise in the front or the middle or the back of our minds that, as Jesus himself told his disciples, God makes absolutely anything possible.

Crucially, the miracle of personal salvation is possible. We can, like the Prodigal Son, turn away from the wreckage of our Godless lives and warm the cockles of our heavenly Father's heart by starting the long or short walk towards home. So many people are homesick for a place they have never seen and find impossible to identify. Because of Jesus they can find that place and one day learn just how loved they are and were, right in the centre of their lostness.

Miracles of healing are possible. We get confused and puzzled and angry and passionate and dogmatic and despairing about this vexed issue, but the Bible tells us that Jesus responded with compassion to all who were in need. I think he still does. Having said that, I have no idea why only a small number of people are healed through prayer, while many, many more are not. And I absolutely refuse to concede that a sick person who feels a little bit better or a lot more cheerful has been miraculously healed. That isn't what happened when folk in need came to Jesus. He healed them. I would *love* to see the healing hand of God on people's lives as it was seen by the crowds who flocked to hear Jesus, wouldn't you? I pray for that to happen and, in the meantime, I do my best to accept the mystery and to trust that God knows best.

Yes, anything is possible because of the resurrection, and that is very good news indeed for us human beings, lumbered as we are with options that, without the power of the Holy Spirit, are dismally finite. Thank God for the miracles that happen in our lives, the ones we know about and, rather importantly, the ones that we were never even aware of.

I follow Jesus because ...
he doesn't do miracles

There must be people who are sick of reading about how I gave up smoking. (No, don't stop reading if you're a smoker – I'm talking about me, not getting at you.) But it is a very good example of what I'm trying to say in this section, so forgive me if I mention it briefly.

Sixteen years ago I was smoking 60 cigarettes a day. I knew I should stop, and I hoped that God would lift the problem painlessly out of my life. He'd done it for one or two others I knew. He didn't do it for me – thank God! When I was closest to giving in he almost certainly stepped in to top up my willpower just a tad, but that's all. Having to grit my teeth through nine months of absolute misery before the pressure eased was one of the most useful and constructive things that has ever happened to me. And, of course, God knew it would be. Like a parent allowing a child space in which to grow, our heavenly Father will sometimes stand back and let us amaze ourselves with our own baby-like achievements, simply because that character-building experience is very good for those of us who are programmed for failure. And when that's the divine intention, looking for short cuts is a waste of time.

Even as I write I'm reminded of something quite ridiculous that happened in our house the other day. How can I even begin to describe it to you? Well, I'll try. There's a game we have often played during long car journeys with bored children (and adults). This is what happens. One person describes a strange or bizarre scenario, and the others have to discover how the situation has come about. The guessers are only allowed to ask 'yes' or 'no' questions. Let me give you an example.

A man enters a saloon in the Wild West and walks up to the bar. A few seconds later the bartender suddenly whips a rifle out from under the counter and threatens the customer with it. There is a short silence, after which the customer expresses his sincere thanks for what the bartender has done. Why? What's going on?

The answer, if you can bear to hear it, is that the customer was suffering from a bad attack of hiccups. The bartender, knowing that a shock can often be an effective cure for this particular complaint, takes his rifle out and frightens the man into an instant cure. Silly, isn't it? But it does take people quite a long time to arrive at the truth when the only answers they're allowed are 'yes' or 'no', and those of us who have experienced the way in which cars can turn into red-hot ovens of discord and discontent will agree that even half an hour of harmony can be extremely welcome.

So, that's the game. You may have played it yourselves. You may be saying, 'Oh, yes, we've been using that boring old hiccup story for years.' Okay, well, now I'll present you with the challenge of this real-life situation that happened just a few days ago in my house. Here is the scenario.

Four people (I am one quarter of them) are roaming impatiently around the various rooms of the house, including the attached double garage. All of us are whistling the first line of the tune of 'Yankee Doodle Dandy', and all of us are becoming increasingly irritable. Every now and then one of us will stop and play the same note on the piano in the living room as the last person who passed through, before continuing on our whistling, irritable way. There you are. What was going on? See if you can work it out before reading the answer in the next paragraph.

Did you guess it? If your mind has turned to *keys* you're definitely on the right track. We were searching for the keys to our car, and if it hadn't been for the fact that we were already miserably late for the theatre I suppose it might have been hilariously funny.

My son's girlfriend, noting the sad and daily consistency with which we misplaced our keys, had very kindly bought us one of those key-ring attachments that are supposed to whistle back to *you* when you whistle to *them*. The theory is excellent, and there may well be versions of this appliance on the market that do faithfully perform exactly that function. Ours was not one of those. On the evening in question we were, unusually, all dressed and ready to go in good time to get to the theatre for the opening of the play. Our sole remaining task was to find the car keys. The general atmosphere as we searched was a pleasantly light and jovial one at first. This time it was going to be easy. After all, we only had to whistle a bit, the thing on the key-ring would chirp back at us, and that would be that.

Without experiencing it, you can have no conception of the speed with which you run out of the will and wetness essential for continuous whistling. Our confident, strident blasts quickly faded into thin, reedy piping sounds as we tried in vain to locate the missing keys. The original light and optimistic atmosphere turned into one of glum frustration, coupled with a growing sense that we were behaving like a bunch of demented loons.

This was nothing compared to what followed. Someone suggested we should dig out the packaging that our non-whistling thing had come in, and check we were doing it right. We found it – without whistling. The instructions, printed on shiny paper in a sub-Lilliputian font, were couched in that strange version of English that results from someone translating with a Chinese–English dictionary and no understanding of grammar. The most important piece of information, however, was quite clear. Unbelievably, the only way of getting the infernal thing to respond was to whistle the first line of 'Yankee Doodle Dandy'. After a moment of stunned silence three of us rushed off to whistle 'Yankee Doodle Dandy' all over the house, only to be arrested by a strangled cry from the person who had been reading the instructions on the packet and was busy deciphering the next bit.

'We have to whistle it in the key of C!' she screamed. 'It has to be in C!'

A stampede began in the direction of the piano, until we realized that only one of us actually needed to play the note. Thereafter, for 10 minutes or more, four relatively sane adults flew around the house whistling 'Yankee Doodle Dandy' in the key of C, fantasizing as they went about applying fiendish tortures to fleshy parts of the Chinaman who had devised the useless gadget that was still failing to respond to their wild but accurately pitched whistles.

The stupid thing never did whistle back at us, and we never did get to the theatre. We found the keys much later in a pile of gunge at the bottom of the kitchen waste bin where Bridget had accidentally dropped them earlier in the day. I washed them, and then whistled 'Yankee Doodle Dandy' in the key of C an inch away from the thing that was supposed to whistle back. It still didn't. I detached it from the keys, took it outside and smashed it with my heel. As I did so, it emitted one tiny and, to my mind, slightly sarcastic whistle.

Can you see now why this ludicrous little story reminded me irresistibly of those occasions, like my desire to give up smoking, when spiritual short cuts look more attractive than personal discipline. Take it from me, like the thing that was supposed to compensate for our lack of organization by whistling back, if God doesn't want it to happen that way, it won't work.

I follow Jesus because ...
**I want to be more like people I've met
who are humble about themselves, make others
feel so much better about *them*selves and are
so proud of belonging to him**

Does your heart warm to humble people? Mine does. Are you humble yourself? I am, despite countless, obvious reasons to be otherwise. Does it not strike you as strange that one as gifted as I should have succeeded in achieving such a correspondingly high level of modesty?

Seriously, though, I'm sure you would agree that true humility is an exceptionally attractive virtue. I'm too fundamentally insecure ever to be one of the life-enhancing folk who possess this quality, but I have met a few during my life, and those encounters have always done me good.

During the course of our second trip to Australia, for instance, I met a man named Peter, who had spent the whole of his working life as a Methodist minister to various churches in different parts of the state of Queensland, and was now on the point of retiring at the age of 65. Peter was cleverer, more sensitive and demonstrably more experienced than I am ever likely to become, and yet he had that very rare and special gift of making the people with whom he came in contact feel far better about themselves than they usually did. As we drove along in his car towards the church where he had invited me to speak, I could feel my confidence opening and blossoming like a flower in the gentle rain of his affirmative manner.

'I cannot tell you,' he said, sounding like an excited small boy, 'how *thrilled* everyone is about you coming to talk to us tonight, and how grateful we are to God for enabling you and Bridget to travel right across the world to bring such a special ministry to us needy Aussies.'

It made me feel like crying. Not, I hasten to add, because I altogether accepted what he was saying, much as I lapped it up like a thirsty little doggy, but because the spirit of the man, inhabited for so many years by the Spirit of God, was so warm and loving and therefore empowering. Because, you see, he meant it! This warm stream of support and appreciation wasn't issuing from one of those irksome individuals who create opportunities for failure by randomly exercising what they call a 'ministry of encouragement' on all and sundry, but from someone whose heart had become, in the best sense, like that of a little child. I found myself actively looking forward to being able to see the smile on Peter's face as I spoke later that evening.

As it happens, my most vivid memory of Peter's inherent humility is connected with something quite practical. A little later during that same journey, the heat inside the car began to be almost unbearable. Summer in Queensland is a blazing affair in which the heat of the sun hits you like a hammer from dawn to dusk. The temperature inside Peter's car had risen to a level which I found very uncomfortable indeed. When I commented on it he must have seen how much I was suffering.

'Look, Adrian,' he said, as though I'd offered to do *him* a favour, 'I – er – I've got just a little bit of air-conditioning down here,' and, taking his left hand from the wheel, he pressed the square button on the dashboard marked A/C to bring what I always think of as a miracle of chilled air swirling through the inside of the vehicle within minutes.

The thing that moved me and made me chuckle inwardly to myself as we drove on was my companion's reluctance to claim an atom of kudos or credit, even for a thing as impersonal and practical as the air-conditioning system in his car. Peter did not have air-conditioning. Peter had 'just a *little bit* of air-conditioning'. I hope you can understand why the addition of those few words had such an effect on me.

Now, the interesting thing about humble Christians like Peter is that, while they may be very self-effacing and generous in giving ground to others, they are by no means pushovers in matters of fundamental standards of behaviour, nor do they compromise the faith that has been responsible for nurturing the fine qualities they possess.

Peter was known in church circles as a man whose single-minded determination to follow Jesus, combined with sheer toughness of spirit, had enabled amazing things to happen in the congregations he had led over the years.

I used to find it very strange that Saint Paul appeared to be boasting openly in his letters to the young churches, but I have begun to realize that there is a proper pride that may and, indeed, *should* be felt by those who are as deeply subsumed into the will of Christ as my friend Peter, or the apostle Paul.

It's a justified and entirely legitimate pride in the God who loves them so much and has gone to such lengths to set them free. And we Christians do indeed have a reason to boast, not about ourselves, but about Jesus, who is our Saviour, our brother, our friend and our God. A great number of the Christians that I meet, and I have been one of them, don't walk with their heads held high, because they're so conscious of the extent to which they fall short of God's highest expectations. I can assure you that if the height at which I held *my* head depended on that comparison there would have to be a special ditch dug (like the ones they used to dig for tall female Hollywood stars who were playing opposite Alan Ladd) so that I could slither miserably along below ground level – or possibly I might have to learn to walk on my hands. Not one of us can walk tall on the basis of our own merits. We all fall dismally short of the glory of God.

But here is the important question. Will we be humble enough to be proud of the one who sets that uncompromising target? Will we lift our eyes and our chins as we march because we're filled with the warm, exciting, energizing knowledge that we belong to him and that he has rescued us from the Egypt of our old lives to be with him for ever, justified and protected, not by our own efforts, but by the blood of his son, Jesus? This is not hollow religious talk – it's the basis for everything that we do.

I meet so many Christians whose progress is paralysed by the low opinion they have of themselves. If you're one of those people, then here's a suggestion. Pack your low opinion at the bottom of a small rucksack (in case you need it later when real pride sets in), give yourself a little shake, stick your chin out and, like my friend Peter, walk humbly behind Jesus with your head held high.

I follow Jesus because ... he knows that evil smells often have a very ordinary origin

They say some stories are better left untold. The one I'm about to narrate is probably a good example of the genre. I was surprised when the person concerned gave me permission to tell it because, frankly, it doesn't show him in his best light. Indeed, immediately after the events I shall shortly describe, he begged me to tell no one what had happened. As well as being surprised I was pleased, because the story is a living example of how 'spiritual excess' can get us into trouble if we haven't checked our facts.

Here, then, is the true, cautionary tale of an evil smell.

One dark afternoon in winter the telephone rang. It was my friend Henry. Henry and I were both Christians, and had known each other for several years. Our close, almost brotherly relationship was punctuated by the occasional mild disagreement, but basically we were fond of each other. Henry's Christian walk was a tumultuous affair, swinging from wild, hectoring assurance to darkest despair and creeping doubt. Recently his state had been one of total assurance, a condition that was slightly wearying for his friends, but infinitely preferable to the mood of crumbling disillusionment that seemed to overwhelm him at other times. On the phone I detected an odd mixture of excitement and worry in his voice.

'Ah, Adrian, you're in. There's, er, a bit of a problem down here.'

'At your house, you mean?'

'Here, yes, that's right, and I'm not quite sure what to do.'

'Well, what's going on?'

'There's a smell in our house.'

I was silent for a moment. I knew nothing about plumbing and it was difficult to see how I could be more qualified than Henry himself to advise on any other kind of household odour.

'A smell?'

'Yes, a smell, but – not just any old smell.'

'Not just—'

'It's an *evil* smell, and I'm talking evil with a capital E.'

I was tempted to say something foolish, but a certain tension in my friend's manner made me check myself.

'Henry, where is this – this evil smell coming from?'

'That's what's so strange,' replied Henry, his voice trembling very slightly. 'When you go into one of the bedrooms it's there. Then, when you go into the bathroom it follows you. Then, if you go into the bedroom again, it follows you back!'

'Hmm, I see. Worrying. What have you done so far?'

'Well, I phoned Doris.'

Doris was an elderly Christian lady living nearby. She had a sizeable reputation for mystical insight and discernment, and had been contacted more than once by local people confronted with what appeared to be spiritual manifestations of the more *outré* type.

'What did she say?'

'She said she'd pray about it and ring back, and when she rang back she said she felt it was very serious and I ought to say the Lord's Prayer in every room of the house.'

'And – and you've done that, have you?'

'Yes, I've done that.'

'And the smell's still there?'

'Yes, it is. I wondered if I ought to get some of the elders round to pray and cast out—'

'Henry,' I interrupted, '*please* don't do anything else until I've been round. I'll be there in about five minutes. Don't ring *anyone* else until I get there.'

When I arrived at Henry's house a few minutes later he immediately showed me upstairs and into one of the children's bedrooms. Sure enough, after a few moments the air filled with a horrible smell that, though faintly familiar, I couldn't quite identify, nor track to a single source.

'Now,' said Henry excitedly, 'come into the bathroom.'

The same vile odour was undoubtedly present a few feet away in the bathroom, but much less strongly than in the bedroom.

'Now come back into the bedroom,' urged Henry, 'and you'll see what I mean.'

As we stepped across the landing and back into the bedroom I found that the smell had abated considerably. Within seconds, however, it had increased to exactly the same pungently unpleasant level as before. I peeled my jacket off and threw it out onto the landing.

'I'm going to take this place to pieces, Henry,' I said.

And I did. I pulled open every drawer and every cupboard, and emptied everything out of them. I shifted every piece of furniture that could be moved and one that theoretically couldn't. I didn't believe in the supposed supernatural origins of that infernal smell and I was determined to prove my instincts right.

After a quarter of an hour no dead rats or rotting pieces of meat had been unearthed, and the smell was worse than ever. It really did seem to be *everywhere* in the room. I sat back on my heels, mopped my brow, and gazed at the ceiling in puzzlement.

I think the truth must have dawned on Henry and I at almost exactly the same moment. He was standing in the centre of the room, immediately beneath the lightshade. I was staring in the same direction, still seeking inspiration. Suddenly everything clicked into place – the fact that it was one of those dark winter days, Henry's deep dislike for wasting money, the feeling that the smell was everywhere in the room at once, the particular fishiness of that loathsome odour – it all made sense!

'It's the light fitting,' said Henry.

And it was. A plastic fitting had somehow slipped down until it was in contact with the glass collar of the burning bulb. Henry's evil smell was the result.

'But why did it seem to follow me…?'

Henry stopped speaking as he mentally answered his own question. On leaving the bedroom each time he had conscientiously switched the light off to save electricity, even when he was only crossing the landing to the bathroom. As a result the plastic stopped burning until the light was switched on once more, thus giving the impression, when he returned, that the smell arrived in the room at almost the same time as he did.

He looked at me, a hunted expression on his face. I knew what he was thinking. He was thinking about his call to Doris, her response, his saying of a prayer in each room of the house, his call to me and our lengthy and energetic search.

'Would you mind,' he said nervously, twisting his fingers together, 'not mentioning this to anyone?'

'No,' I said, with sinful reluctance, 'no, of course I wouldn't mind.'

Henry learned a lesson on that day, and so, I can assure you, did I.

I follow Jesus because ... in his world, love comes first

We had just moved house, and for the first time since I began to be a professional writer I had a study, my very own little kingdom. It wasn't a large room; in fact it was quite small, with a little walk-in storage cupboard to one side, but, as I delighted in telling friends who dropped in to look around, it was *mine*. It belonged to me. It was a place dedicated to my use. It wasn't anyone else's. It didn't belong to another person. It was exclusively earmarked for the work that I did. It was *mine*. If I could have thought of another 35 ways of expressing that succulent fact, I would have used them to bore my friends to death at an even faster rate than usual. I was *so* happy to have my own space.

One of the first things I did on acquiring my citadel was to hunt through all our books (some were unpacked and on shelves, many were still in the cardboard boxes we used for the move) to find all the 'comfort books' that have meant so much to me throughout my life. These included children's books, particularly the 'Just William' series by Richmal Crompton, humorous works by giants of literary comedy like P. G. Wodehouse and Jerome K. Jerome, several C. S. Lewis favourites, and a whole other widely varying selection of writings that have enriched my life in one way or another. They're a shabby, overbrowsed bunch all-in-all, a few very unwisely read in the bath, but, for the first time, they were all standing richly together on rows of shelves beside the door, and just behind me as I sat at my desk. No longer would they have to be hunted down with the mounting fury and diminishing patience that has become my very own special trademark.

Because, you see, they were *mine*, and they were in *my* study.

I really enjoyed setting my desk up as well. On the left-hand corner at the back stood the white anglepoise lamp that I switch on every morning before starting work, however dark or light the morning might be – nowadays that small action seems to correspond with switching my brain on in some strange way. In the centre of my desk stood the computer, the one I mentioned earlier that's frequently rude to me, and on the right stood the printer. The printer is in league with the computer, but I have its measure now. Discipline is what works with a printer. Be firm. Simply refuse to accept any hint of failure to operate properly. My wife occasionally uses this machine, and regularly has trouble with it because she's too soft. On these occasions she calls me. The moment I appear the cowardly thing flings itself into frantic, chattering, panic-stricken action, hoping to win my approval and avoid a beating. Believe me, you've got to let a printer know who's boss.

At the front of my desk and to the left stood that combination telephone, fax and answering machine I told you about. I endure its leering presence only because I need it so much, but I'm only too aware that it secretly resents finding itself owned by a technological lame-brain like me. Some day the reckoning must come. I'm ready.

In one of the desk drawers beside my chair I squirrelled away a delicious collection of stationery articles which I planned to try very hard never to use. I have always been irresistibly drawn to stationery counters in newsagents' shops. I'm a loony about stationery. I love it all. I love the rubber bands and the sticky labels and the pencil sharpeners and the pencils and the Sellotape and the paperclips and the staple guns and the Blu-Tack and the drawing pins and the neat little packs of envelopes. I love their fiddly, twiddly, functional little beingness, and I love having them stowed away in *my* drawer. Yes, I do! In the other, lower drawer there were just under a million cheap biros. Resigned to the wretchedly shameful fact that every single member of my family is an incurable pen-thief, I asked only that *one* functional pen should be available when I needed it.

On the shelf to my right, a shelf miraculously fixed to the wall for me by a friend who has the Gift of Attachment, there were two things. The first was a little row of reference books. These were, in no particular order, the *Concise Oxford Dictionary*, a *Complete Concordance* of the New International Version of the Bible, H. L. Mencken's *Dictionary of Quotations* and a Chambers paperback *Thesaurus*. It's from these volumes that I frequently haul planks to facilitate crossing the yawning chasms of my thought and creativity. They stand beside me as I write today, sturdy forests of wisdom.

The second thing on the shelf was a pot containing three blooming hyacinth plants, bought for me by my wife. This was an act of profound generosity on her part, knowing as she does that buying a hyacinth for me is the equivalent of sending any other man off to Brighton for a weekend with Pamela Anderson. The way in which I wantonly soak in the scent of hyacinths is positively sinful. (I suppose that should be *negatively* sinful, shouldn't it?) I don't know why it is, but that particular heavenly aroma makes my eyes glaze over with pleasure. You can keep your hash and your Ecstasy – I shall stick to my hyacinths. I rather like the idea of clubs full of people with glazed eyes passing pots of hyacinths around.

Other features of my newly appointed little place of work included the chair I'm now sitting on – firm, yet sufficiently yielding in the seat to become formed by the force of gravity into my individual shape as the months went by, and another seat in the corner, not quite so comfortable, of course, for those who would be granted temporary residence in my kingdom from time to time. Add to all these things the walk-in cupboard where, for the first time in living memory, my files were stored in some kind of easily accessible manner, and you could hardly blame me if I began to feel that it would only really be necessary to leave this place in order to have the odd meal and to sleep.

Isn't it funny how God sends little things to teach you a lesson? I came into my study one morning soon after setting it all up, glanced pleasurably around for a moment or two, yet again relishing the fact that it was all *mine*, and sat down at my desk. I think I really had got a little bit carried away with the way in which the whole thing was so organized and self-contained and geared exclusively to what I wanted. Glancing down to my right, where a recently acquired memo board was leaning against the desk-leg waiting to be attached to the wall, I felt a sudden spasm of annoyance. The day before I had very carefully used my specially purchased, wet-wipe pen to make a list of the tasks that had to be performed on the following day. Some *evil* person had rubbed out my list and written something else instead. I was about to storm out and exact summary revenge on the only likely suspect, my 10-year-old daughter, when I happened to notice what had been written across the white surface of the board.

'IMPORTANT,' it said, in huge capital letters, and then there was a big arrow pointing to just four little words in the corner. So small were they that I had to get down on my hands and knees to see what they said.

'Remember to kiss Katy...'

May God, in his mercy, grant me the humility and wisdom to remember, when I'm obsessed or caught up with my own possessions and concerns and accomplishments, that the demands of love and relationship will always be a first priority in the only kingdom that really matters.

Thank you, Jesus – and Katy.

I follow Jesus because ...
he's less narrow and boring about salvation
than an awful lot of his followers

Who will be saved?

Let's have a little recap of what a question like this might mean before we try to answer it in any detail. Well – let's try, anyway.

Jesus made it clear that a disaster of cosmic proportions, one that our finite minds can only fleetingly grasp, is threatening each human being on this planet. His aim, directed by the profound love of God for mankind, was and is to save as many people as possible from what we rather shyly call 'hell'.

He explained that men and women can indeed be rescued by being figuratively or physically baptized in his name, by declaring their allegiance to him, by following him, by being obedient to him, by making him the first priority in their lives, and by assenting to the proposition that his death on the cross has been graciously regarded by God as a substitute for punishment that they should justly receive. God's act in bringing Jesus back to life after three days loosened the grip of death on humanity, thus defeating the devil, a fallen angel whose ongoing intention is to con-fuse and blind humanity to the truth, so that they cannot enter the heaven he has left and lost for ever. All of these things are, of course, no less true because we don't fully understand them.

The Spirit of God will live in us if we truly follow Jesus. As a result we will become committed to other people's physical and temporal needs, just as Jesus himself was. However, the major issue confronting us is not how we are to pay our rent, nor how we cope with illness, nor has it anything to do with whether we play the lottery or not, important though these things may seem to be or actually are. The major issue, the one we shall all have to face, preferably before death, is that, through Jesus, the love of God offers rich and eternal life with him as opposed to some unspeakably appalling alternative. Nothing is more important than that fact.

Jesus came to save sinners, and he wishes to continue through us, the body of Christ on earth. This, incidentally, is the ultimate reason for following Jesus.

Okay, that's the scenario, so back to the original ques-tion. Who will be saved?

A couple of years ago, soon after the death of Diana, Princess of Wales, some people took exception to a com-ment I made about the likelihood that she had met Jesus by then, and that the most important things in her life would have been resolved. Now, as then, I don't care to waste time defending that statement because, as it literally stands, I'm quite sure that it's absolutely true and thoroughly bibli-cal, but I would like you to join me as I follow my nose in search of some kind of answer to my opening question. I'm very far from being systematic, as more discerning readers may already have noticed, but I feel sure we shall arrive *somewhere*.

Who will be saved?

As we have already mentioned Diana, let us begin with Mother Teresa, who died at almost exactly the same time. Don't you think it was wonderful, first of all, that God managed to slip her out of the back door and home, at the only point in modern history when the ending of her life would be eclipsed by the death of somebody else? The meaning of the parable of her life was confirmed by the manner of her passing. She was not important, but Jesus is.

Now, still hanging on to our initial question, I have just stated that God has taken this remarkable woman home to be with him in heaven.

But has he?

I have recorded elsewhere my meetings with people who countered my enthusiasm about Mother Teresa with the dark words, 'Ah, yes, but is she saved?' What they were really asking, of course, was whether she had gone through the established set of procedures that evangelical Christians have decided is the only respectable path to salvation. Was she aware of the four spiritual laws, and did she proceed accordingly? Did she repent of her sins, asking Jesus into her life to be her Lord and Saviour, and did she confess him before God and men? I haven't the faintest idea whether or not Mother Teresa selected a conversion package that would satisfy the sterner brethren, but I do know some things.

I know that she saw Jesus in the eyes and faces of starving, filthy beggars, and that she cleaned and fed and comforted them because she was doing it for him.

I know that Jesus pointed out in the twenty-fifth chapter of the Gospel of Matthew that it's those who feed him, and quench his thirst, and clothe him, and ask him in when he's a stranger, and look after him when he's sick, and visit him in prison, who will receive the inheritance – the kingdom prepared for them since the creation of the world. And I know, because he said so, that many of those will not even realize that they did it for him. Woe betide us if we arrive at the gates of heaven with a 'perfect' conversion and no loving works.

I know that if I were to arrive at those same gates and find myself behind Mother Teresa in the queue, I would hide behind her skirts and, when some eagle-eyed angel spotted me, tell God she was a friend of mine in the hope that such a claim might influence him.

I know that if Jesus was in hospital he would rather be visited by someone with warmth, humour, kindness, a box of chocolates and a shaky understanding of the things of God, than some miserable character with a perfect theology who was only there out of duty. I recall with blushing horror a much earlier period of my life when, as predatory members of our college Christian Union, we lured members of obscure sects to speak to us under the pretext of wanting to learn about their beliefs, then hacked savagely and triumphantly at them with specially sharpened shards of Scripture when they admitted that they had never invited Jesus into their lives. We showed them a thing or two about the love of God, I can tell you. If you have not love...

Who will be saved?

'Of course,' someone cries, 'those involved in great ministries, those who have healed and cast out devils in the name of Jesus, surely they *must* be saved.' Well, I expect many of them will be, but Jesus makes it quite clear that some so-called followers who present themselves to him with what appear to be perfect credentials on paper will be greeted with those dreadful words, 'I never knew you.'

'Ah, but you don't quite understand,' they'll say, 'we really did do marvellous things in your name. We were leading lights in our church movement. We were – look, we were important!'

'Yes, you were,' Jesus will quietly reply, 'you were very, *very* important, and I never knew you.'

'But we prayed – we prayed! We prayed a lot – loudly. We called on your name every Sunday.'

'You did,' Jesus will say, 'but not all who cry, "Lord, Lord!" will enter the kingdom of heaven, only those who are obedient. I never knew you.'

Who will be saved?

You are dying to say to me that I surely must agree with the proposition that Jesus is the one way to the Father. *Surely* I must agree with that. Yes, I do. Jesus himself said it. Therefore it's certainly true. But Jesus also said that those who give as little as a cup of water to his servants for his sake will receive a reward. What will that reward be? Will it be a weekly day-pass to heaven from hell? Will it be a special concession of air-conditioning in whatever variety of accommodation they occupy in the infernal regions? Or will they be saved? You tell me, because I really don't know.

What will happen to the men who nailed Jesus to the cross? Jesus prayed that his Father would forgive them for what they were doing to him. What is the implication of this prayer for those men? At the tomb of Lazarus Jesus thanked his Father for always hearing and answering his prayers. If the prayer for those who hammered the nails in has been answered, those men are now in heaven. Do you believe that? They weren't even evangelicals, let alone born-again believers. They killed the Son of God. Could it be that Jesus is allowed to be The Way for absolutely anyone he chooses? No, surely not…

Who will be saved?

What about nasty, horrible people who happened to say some sort of prayer of commitment one day, but have slid disastrously away from the path of rectitude and religion ever since? What about them? Are they saved because they said the right words and meant them for three and a half minutes? Or not? What about babies and small children? What about people whose brains don't work properly? What about dogs and cats? What about fleas?

Enough of this nonsense. I have no idea who will be saved and who will not, because it's none of my business. God will save whom he will save. I know the basic spiritual mechanics of salvation just as well as anyone else, but I also know that salvation isn't actually a mechanical process. It's about following and loving Jesus, and if there are any non-Christians reading this, I'd like to point you to that part of the Bible (the twenty-first chapter of the Gospel of John) where Peter suddenly recognizes Jesus on the bank of the Sea of Tiberias, and is so excited that he leaps into the water and splashes his way to the shore to be with him.

Why did Peter rush so precipitately to be with his master when, only a short time before, he had denied him? Why wasn't he too embarrassed to go near him? Was it because he was worried that he might have lost his eternal life and was anxious to get it sorted out? Was it because he was hoping to be given clarification on one or two matters of doctrine about which he felt a little unsure? Was it because he had just formulated a new statement of faith for potential believers and was keen to get it ratified? Was it because he wanted to impart a vision he had just had of the distant future, featuring groups of Christians who were as richly relaxed and kind and caring as their master?

No, it was none of these things. I'll tell you what it was. Peter wanted to be with Jesus because he loved him *so* much, and nothing else in the universe mattered.

But here is a paradox. The more uncertain I become about who is saved and who is not, the more certain I become that I must preach Jesus as the only way. Strange that, isn't it?

Never mind who is saved, unless God has specifically made it our business. Let us fall in love with Jesus and, when the time is right, tell people about him.

I follow Jesus because ... he encourages me to live 'now'

One of our longest-running television programmes is the show called *This Is Your Life*. I don't know exactly when it began, but it must have been shortly after I was born because I can't recall a time when it didn't exist. Most people must surely have seen the programme at least once, but in case you haven't, I'll explain how it works so that you know what I'm talking about.

The general idea of *This Is Your Life* is that some unsuspecting famous or worthy person is ambushed by the presenter of the programme (Eamonn Andrews in the early days – remember him? – or Michael Aspel nowadays) bearing a large red book with the victim's name on it, and hauled off to a studio theatre to have the story of his or her life told in front of a live audience and, of course, vast numbers of television viewers as well. In the following 30 minutes a variety of surprise guests, who may be friends, family or admirers of the subject, make dramatic appearances through the curtains at the back of the stage to share personal anecdotes and memories. The climax of the proceedings tends to be the entrance of some especially significant individual separated by many years or thousands of miles from the star of the show. A tearful reunion followed by swelling music and embraces all round is the final course on the menu of this carefully planned feast of emotion.

In all the years that *This Is Your Life* has been running, I think only a couple of people (the footballer Danny Blanchflower was one) have ever actually refused to be dragged off to have their lives publicly reviewed, but that was two too many embarrassments for the television company concerned, who, after the second such negative encounter, decided that from then on the show would be recorded to avoid the risk of having to fill an empty half hour.

The vast majority of the victims have always seemed more or less to enjoy the experience, and as a child I found it very difficult to understand how they could possibly react in any other way. Just imagine, I thought, having all the people you've ever known turning up one by one to kiss you or shake your hand and tell the whole world how wonderful you are. What more could you possibly ask for? As a rather complex and troubled child, I found the programme becoming, almost unconsciously, a symbol to me of an inner yearning that, one day, everything in my life would sort itself out and I would arrive at some kind of glorious, *This Is Your Life*-like climactic moment in which, with tears of joy, I would discover that all my hurts were healed, all loose ends tied up and all my chronic problems solved.

The absurdity of such a specific notion caused it to fade as the years passed, of course, but for the first 40 years of my life I did remain trapped in the grim prison of believing that true happiness could only lie in the future, and that the things I was doing and experiencing *now* were of such little value that they were hardly worth regarding. What a recipe for the wasting of days!

As I approached my fortieth birthday, I wrote a song for a revue which included the following verse:

And good old Eamonn Andrews
Would come smiling round the corner
With a big red book and people
Who would say, 'We always loved you!'
And you'd wonder why on earth
They never told you when you needed
All the love that they could offer
What a shame
But as he moved towards you
You would know it doesn't matter
As it's just another way
To lose the game that you are playing
For in letters that are golden
On the big red book he'd show you
There is someone else's name
And the dream of being special floats away
And the whole sad world looks so grey.

General pessimism about potential prospects, of which this verse is an obvious symptom, was a bleak but very necessary part of my transition from being someone who relied on phantoms of the future to being someone who is able truly to enjoy the things that are happening to me and around me *today*. The process is by no means completed, but it's well under way.

C. S. Lewis said that, if the world were to become perfect, God would look down and see a man reading a book in a garden. I needed to understand that so-called prosaic or trivial activities happening right now are actually at the heart of real peace and contentment. This awareness might take us a long way towards understanding what Jesus was talking about when he spoke of the kingdom of God actually being among us, and it may also be the key to a special kind of joy that's much deeper and more spiritually nourishing than mere happiness. I suspect that Jesus looked fondly around at the faces of his disciples as they all ate meals together and knew with a sweet mixture of joy and pain that this was as good as it was likely to get on this side of heaven.

These thoughts arose in me on the day following my return from a summer holiday I once spent in France with the other five members of my family. It was a good and enjoyable experience to be away together, despite the occasional (and in our case seemingly inevitable) arguments and tensions, but two things particularly spring to mind in connection with the things that I have just been saying.

The first was a couple of hours spent in the beautiful forest on the hills overlooking a little cottage in Normandy where we stay quite often. We took bicycles with us on the back of the car to ride along the tree-lined tracks, a rug to sit on, a ball to throw, a bottle of orange squash to drink, a big bag of crisps to eat and a book to read. As we sat in the dappled coolness of the cathedral-like forest, throwing our ball to each other and listening as Katy (aged 11 at the time) read to us, I very nearly managed to allow *now* to be eternal.

The other occasion was earlier in the holiday, when we were staying at a place much further south, quite near to the wonderful city of Chartres. Four of us hired putters and golf balls so that we could play on one of the Crazy Golf courses that the French seem so keen on. We were the only people there because a light rain was falling, and it turned out to be one of those God-given times when the silliest things seem screamingly funny and you don't care whether you win or lose and the weather can do what it likes. We were people who loved each other, being happy for an hour. For me, at least, nothing else mattered. When we returned to the place where we were staying, I wrote the first poem I had written for quite a long time:

There is not much more
Need not be more
Than playing Crazy Golf in France
Laughing in the summer rain.

Sufficient unto the day is the evil thereof – the good as well, one suspects. Thank God for the *now*.

I follow Jesus because ...
he's more interested in what happens behind the scenes than in my public posing

I travel frequently to Europe – sorry, I mean to other parts of our great brotherhood of nations. A small but important lesson made one journey particularly memorable.

This trip was already different from others I had done in one significant way. A Christian television company, based in the United Kingdom and calling itself Christian Television Associates, had decided that they would like to make what is sometimes called a 'fly-on-the-wall' documentary programme about the wide variety of work and leisure activity that fills up a year of my life. As you know, the 'fly-on-the-wall' aspect simply means that the television cameras record what happens both formally and informally, as opposed to concentrating only on specially prepared and presented set pieces. By the time I had experienced the continual presence of a TV camera probing every intimate corner of my existence for only a month or so, I frequently found myself wanting to roll up one of the heavier quality newspapers in order to swat this 'fly', and I think I would have done exactly that on the trip I want to tell you about if the CTA camera operator who accompanied me hadn't been as likeable as he was infuriating.

Crawford Telfor is a Glaswegian distinguished by his small stature, extraordinarily bad jokes and incredibly thick skin, who once worked for the BBC but is now a director of Christian Television Associates. He was waiting for me as I walked up to the Lufthansa check-in desk at Gatwick Airport, armed and ready to poke his lens into every crack and cranny of my bleary-eyed progress towards the plane that was scheduled to take both of us to Stuttgart in an hour's time.

The girl on the check-in desk was amused but faintly nervous to find that her security-related questions were being recorded for posterity, but many of the other passengers in the terminal were completely gobsmacked as I approached them pushing a luggage trolley containing not cases and bags, but Crawford, lying on his back with his feet in the air, filming upwards in order to get an interestingly angled view of my face as I approached the departure gates. Don't ask me why I let him do that. I just don't know.

On the plane itself things got worse. Crawford was determined to film me actually arriving at my seat and depositing my hand luggage in the overhead locker. This he proceeded to do, much to the annoyance of a fellow passenger, who strongly resented access to her own seat being used as a vantage point for my little one-man camera team, who, for all she knew, was simply co-operating in the production of a ludicrously egocentric amateur holiday video.

'Is this really essential?' she enquired in acid tones.

I wanted to die. Crawford calmly filmed me wanting to die, and continued filming from his seat by the window as I ate my airline snack, read my airline magazine and dozed my airline doze. Finally, I cracked. I couldn't stand it any more. Turning to face the camera lens, I spoke in low, ominous tones.

'If you don't take that camera out of my face,' I threatened, 'I shall insert it so far into you that you'll require microsurgery to remove it.'

He lowered his camera for an instant. 'I didn't quite get the beginning of that,' he said. 'Would you mind just repeating it…?'

Over the next 24 hours it didn't get much better, but the next day I got my own back a little when we ate lunch in a Japanese restaurant with Christian Rendell, a splendid fellow who translates my books and interprets for me when I speak in Germany. This was one of those Japanese restaurants where the centre of the table at which you sit to eat is also the metal hotplate on which the meal is cooked. Having ordered our dishes from a waitress, we sat and waited for the chef to complete his work for diners on a table at the other end of the restaurant before coming to ours.

Needless to say, Crawford had already checked with the manageress of the establishment that filming was allowed, but for some reason this information had failed to filter through to the chef. When he did finally arrive, Crawford happened to have put his camera down and was sitting quietly, looking strangely naked but reasonably normal for once. Our cook was a very impressive figure, far from tall, but intensely serious in manner, dressed in pristinely white garments and surmounted by an unusually tall chef's hat, which lent immense dignity to his slight figure. At his waist hung a leather belt, cunningly designed to accommodate a range of lethal-looking metal cooking implements of varying length and design.

With nimble-fingered skill and a hiss of frying ingredients, this master of the oriental arts began to slice, turn, mix and flavour the combination of rice, chicken and prawns that would shortly become our lunch. Christian and I were concentrating hungrily on the culinary process, but out of the corner of my eye I did notice that, predictably, Crawford's hand was stealing down towards the camera that lay on the floor beside him. Seconds later he was on his feet, eye firmly against the viewfinder, circling and advancing on the chef from behind, so that, eventually, the long lens was actually pointing down over the little man's shoulder and beside his face towards the food that he was preparing.

I cannot tell what the chef thought this thing was that had suddenly appeared over his right shoulder, but I shall never forget his reaction to the sight. In the best Samurai tradition he sprang back into a defensive posture, a loud, guttural cry of shock and aggression issuing from his throat. He lifted the implement that happened to be in his hand at the time as though seriously intending to impale Crawford on the end of it.

You have to give it to my small Scottish friend (and someone nearly did on this occasion) – his ubiquitous camera-work may have been intensely irritating, but he is courageous to the point of near death. Not only did he continue filming, but I could have sworn that he moved a little closer, presumably hoping to get a really good close-up of the murderous expression on his assailant's face as the blow landed.

All of us, including Crawford, survived this experience, although the chef took a little while to calm down, and Christian, who regards Japanese restaurants as sacred temples of Epicurean delight, was deeply embarrassed.

Over the next three days Crawford continued to be a constant presence. We got used to him and his camera in the same way that you get used to a small wound that refuses to heal properly. He filmed Christian driving, me sleeping in the back of the car, both of us eating, several members of the public minding their own business, and a bit of countryside. When we crossed the border into Holland he filmed my translator's wife offering her opinion that the nicest part of England was Scotland, he filmed me getting annoyed with my Dutch publisher because the cartoon on the cover of my latest book made me look like an alcoholic barrage balloon, and finally he asked if he could do some recording in the hotel room where I stayed on the night before flying back to England the next morning.

By then I felt genuinely exhausted, and when Crawford pointed his camera at me as I lay flopped on the bed and asked me why I do what I do when it gets so tiring, I found it very difficult to produce a coherent answer.

It was when I was waiting to go to sleep a little later that the significance of Crawford's eternal 'thereness' really struck me. I pay general lip service to the idea that the eyes of God are always on me, but the fact of that camera pointing relentlessly at me when I wasn't in the public view as well as when I was standing and bleating behind a microphone was leading me to wonder just how much of a reality the presence of God was for me. After all, I reflected, when the time comes to face my maker, and he announces that we're to watch a heavenly video rerun of my life, he's likely to fast-forward the public performances and concentrate on the fly-on-the-wall stuff.

'So what it amounts to,' I muttered to God just before I fell asleep, 'is that if I want to follow you there's no such thing as being "off duty". That's hard, God, that's very hard, but I do see your point.'

As I drifted into unconsciousness, I could have sworn that I heard the voice of a small Scottish angel saying, 'Would you mind thinking that thought just one more time…?'

I follow Jesus because ...
he helped me to write him back into my life

Every now and then, after a talk, or in the course of a workshop, someone will ask me if any of the things that I write have been directly inspired by God. My answer never varies very much. I don't believe that the things I produce are any more or less directly inspired than, let's say, a specific leg of lamb selected by a Christian butcher to buy and chop up and sell to his customers. Please don't misunderstand me. I certainly hope that God approves of my stuff. I continually ask him to make sure that I avoid the temptation to get too carried away on unproductive or harmful flights of fancy. I pray for those who read the platoons of sentences that come marching out of my mind, that they may feel just a little warmer towards Jesus as a result of what meets their eyes. I do all these things, but were you to ask if the Holy Spirit sits on a stool next to me, dictating every word of the text, I should have to reply firmly in the negative, cosy though such an arrangement might appear. I'm glad really. I think I might get rather bored with the post of God's full-time stenographer.

If, on the other hand, you were to ask if God uses my material – well, there we're definitely talking about something else. God, as you know, is a great opportunist. He happily seems to use any old rubbish when nothing else is available. And you can't predict the post by looking at the postman, so – yes, the Holy Spirit does sometimes speak to people through my words. Thank God he does. What a privilege that is.

Now, having said all this, I want to tell you about an occasion when the content of my writing was so infused by the spiritual battle raging for my soul, that I might have been excused for beginning to wonder if the divine hand was placed upon my own as it moved across the page. And the extraordinary thing about it is that this was one of the very first things I wrote. It's called *The Visit*.

The Visit is a story in six short parts, and it concerns the unexpected return to a very ordinary High Street church of the 'Founder', a figure who is clearly meant to be Jesus, though he's never actually named during the story. The first part of the story was written in the early 1980s, at a time when, although neither my wife nor I were aware of it, I was heading for a stress-related illness that was to change the course of my life. One evening Bridget and I were sitting in front of the television after the children had gone to bed, when, quite abruptly, I had an idea for a story. It was an idea that filled me up with itself. It choked me. It took my breath away. As it developed in my mind I began to feel an absurd concern that if I moved my body too abruptly the whole thing would somehow be spilled and lost. Finally, I switched off the television and asked Bridget to find writing paper and a pen so that I could dictate something to her. Taking a pad of lined paper to the dining table at the other end of the room, she sat down and looked expectantly in my direction.

The next 30 minutes or so turned out to be one of the strangest, most intense half hours of my life. Fuelled, as I perceive in retrospect, by a desperate desire to establish the reality of Jesus at a time when that reality seemed to be drifting away, the story poured out in a stream that remained unabated until the last word was safely down on the page. Both of us were in tears throughout the process. At the end we were emotionally exhausted and rather puzzled by the experience, but we did sense that something important had happened. Unlike almost everything else I have written since, I hardly altered a comma or restructured a sentence in subsequent drafts, and I wouldn't think of doing so now. The style has a freshness and immediacy that's very hard to recapture in these days when my writing has become a source of income, and my style suffers as much as it benefits from professional objectivity.

The rest of *The Visit* was written a year or two later, as I was beginning to emerge from the aforementioned illness. Indeed, those who knew me well at that time might easily trace the path of my spiritual and emotional fragmentation as it winds through the landscape of those additional five sections. The writing of this extra material wasn't accompanied by the same intensity as the first part, but there were some memorably odd moments. The fifth story, for instance, concerns a crucial choice needing to be made by the man who, throughout *The Visit*, is narrating his experiences with the Founder. Basically, his choice is between good and evil – between physically following Jesus or being drawn away by a strange, shadowy figure approximating, I suppose, to the devil. I wrote the first half of the story, the part leading up to the point where this choice had to be made, during the morning and then left it, intending to continue on the following day. However, our house seemed to be filled with darkness and oppression that afternoon and evening, and Bridget, who had read my output for the day, suggested that until I had finished the story in a satisfactory way, there would be no peace for us. I did finish it, and she was right. I don't attempt to explain that sequence of events. I simply record it as further evidence that there was something oddly significant about this particular piece of work.

Eventually *The Visit* was published in Britain as part of a book called *The Final Boundary*, a collection of short stories that appeared immediately in the wake of *The Sacred Diary of Adrian Plass*. I was very proud of *The Final Boundary*, but quite a lot of potential readers were thrown by its appearance immediately after such an apparently very different book. Why wasn't I producing another three dozen volumes in the *Sacred Diary* mould? After all, that was what usually happened when a book was successful. Perhaps because of this reaction, *The Visit* was somewhat lost over the following years in this country, although it has always had a real popularity with those who happened to discover it. For years, Bridget had been urging me to find a way to make these stories available to more people in an accessible and attractive form, and in 1999, to our great excitement, that's exactly what happened.

As we approached the millennium, *The Visit*, a book about Jesus returning to his own, was published by HarperCollins as a large-format book with superb illustrations by Ben Ecclestone, also my collaborator on such projects as *Learning to Fly* and *Words from the Cross*. Words cannot describe the pleasure with which I saw these plans come to fruition. *The Visit* is a crucial part of my personal history, an important hinge on which my life turned. God didn't write it, but, in some indefinable way, he certainly seemed to stand over me to make sure I got it right, and in the writing of those words I remembered who I had met and why I had become a Christian all those years ago.

And the central message of the book? Well, it concerns the forthcoming and decidedly nonfictional return of Jesus, and was the same when this century began as when the story was written in the 1980s: Would you be ready?

I follow Jesus because …
he forgives me for sins I'm not even aware of,
for being extremely silly, and for sometimes
being very annoying to other people

It's funny, isn't it, how we Christians talk mainly about the more cataclysmic sins, when the faults that actually beset us most are either ones we're not even aware of, or else are scratchy little offences that seem hardly dignified enough to talk about or confess. Let me give you an example of each.

Example 1

First of all, there are the sins or failings that we don't notice in ourselves. Take self-delusion, for instance.

Have you ever found yourself engaged in conversation with someone who suddenly says something that completely robs you of the power of speech? There was a time when this happened to me twice over a period of a few weeks, and on both occasions for more or less the same reason.

The first was in the course of a celebratory meal of some kind, when I was sitting next to a man whom I shall call Ronald. Ronald is famous – well, infamous, really – in our immediate circle for his tendency to say hurtful and insensitive things to friends and acquaintances. Inwardly blessing my hostess for deliberately placing me beside such a delightful dinner companion, I was doing my very best to make pleasant conversation when Ronald adroitly turned the subject to a mutual friend called Jill, who happened to be sitting further down the table.

'I'm very fond of Jill, of course,' said Ronald, leaning towards my ear and lowering his voice so that nobody else could hear, 'but don't you get a bit annoyed by the way she talks to people sometimes? I know I do.'

Conscious that my mouth had started to open and close like a goldfish out of water, I tried to say something, but the words wouldn't come.

'The thing is,' continued Ronald, warming to his theme, 'I've always thought that an important part of being a Christian is making sure that you don't hurt other people by the things you say. I'm *very* careful myself.'

My mouth no longer opened and closed – it just hung open. I stared blankly at Ronald as he developed his argument.

'I never say anything that's likely to upset the person I'm speaking to,' he explained. 'That's how I manage to maintain such good relationships with everybody I know.'

Just for a moment I wondered if he might be making a joke at his own expense. Could it really be possible that this was the same Ronald who had once said to me, 'My poems are about things that appear trivial to everybody else,' and had then, without drawing a breath, announced that he had written a poem about *me?* Was he seriously claiming to be scrupulously aware of the way in which his words might affect others? I peered hopefully into his eyes, hoping to detect the merest sparkle of self-mockery somewhere in their depths. Not a flicker could I see.

'B-but...' I began, then gave up, aware that this was probably not an ideal situation in which to revolutionize Ronald's view of himself as the most tactful person in the universe. In any case, I don't think he would have believed me. Was Ronald going mad? No, but he was seriously self-deluded.

The same sort of thing happened no more than a fortnight later. A very close friend called Julia came for coffee and, in the course of our chat, informed Bridget and me that she disapproved strongly of those parents who make a regular habit of complaining to the local school about the way in which their children are treated. This time we *both* sat there with our mouths hanging open. Bridget recovered first.

'But, Julia,' she said gently, 'you've been up to the school to complain ever so many times since your two started going, haven't you?'

A look of mystification and slight annoyance appeared on Julia's face. 'No I haven't,' she replied. 'I've hardly ever been up there – once or twice, perhaps, but certainly no more than that.' She shook her head in puzzlement. 'I really don't know what you mean.'

Bridget and I exchanged glances. How many times over the last few years, we silently asked each other, have we sat in this very room listening to Julia's latest account of how she 'went up that school' and gave them a piece of her mind that they wouldn't forget in a hurry? Many times, we silently answered each other – too many times to count. Were we going mad? Was Julia going mad? No, but she was terribly self-deluded.

I mention these two incidents because they set up a small but persistently worrying question in the back of my mind. It was very easy for me to conclude that Ronald and Julia were deluded about those aspects of their behaviour that I have mentioned, but what about me? Do I sometimes confidently assert that I *never* do this and *always* do that, while others listen with incredulous, dumb disbelief?

Having considered this question carefully, I'm absolutely sure that, in fact, I *never* do such a thing – but, on the other hand, it's just possible that I'm chronically self-deluded. How about you?

Example 2

Secondly, there are the petty, silly little things that can cause real annoyance to other people. I feel myself blushing as I enter the confessional.

It was late December, and Christmas fever was upon us all once more. The change of atmosphere in the streets and shops was as pronounced and difficult to define as ever. People went about their business with just a little more briskness than usual, and there was a heightened sense of excitement as life flowed, like water in an emptying bath, towards the plughole of that single, confusedly significant day.

In case any of you think that the image I have just employed is wholly inappropriate to the blessed season of Advent, all I can say is that it was absolutely in line with the way I was feeling at that particular time. The preceding 12 months had been one of the busiest years I had known for a long time, and I was running out of steam. I thanked God for the work, but I couldn't wait for the new year to come, because, in 1998, I was planning to take a whole year off from all public speaking and performance. This was happening for a number of reasons, not least among which was the fact that I was simply sick of the sound of my own voice. I intended to spend a year writing more material and actually *living* life, rather than seeing it as a series of repeatable anecdotes.

Another part of my motivation was connected with an observation that Christian initiatives and ministries never actually seemed to end. Have you noticed that? They either dribble away into nothingness, or they're enshrined inflexibly and eternally in a form that's quite often a travesty of the original. Or sometimes those involved continue to go miserably through the motions, assuming that lack of finance, support or any visible success is some test of faithfulness imposed upon them by the Lord. I intended to use my free year to check that God really did want me to continue with the things I had been doing, in the way that I had been doing them. I hoped that those who had been displeased by my writings would pray with particular faith-fulness that the Holy Spirit would make it clear to me that they were right. And, of course, I had absolutely no objec-tion to those who liked what I wrote throwing up the occasional prayer as well. Just in case I was right, you understand…

Yes, I was certainly looking forward to it. It should be good. For a whole year I would be a 'local person', a regular attender at my own church, a person who made family plans for the weekend. I would still be writing, but that was more like a 'proper job' anyway. I was really relishing the prospect.

In the meantime, however, as I said just now, I was running out of 'oomph', and getting mean and petty and irritable as a result.

One day I had to walk into town to post a parcel and some letters. Quite apart from my general feelings of tired-ness and harassment, I had been obliged to wrap a parcel before coming out, an activity which has always reduced me to teeth-clenching, quivering fury within minutes of starting. Why *can't* I do it? Why *can* others do it? Why do rolls of Sellotape, pairs of scissors and sheets of brown paper start distorting themselves and sticking to the wrong things and leaping about and misbehaving like delinquents in a bottom-set maths class as soon as I come anywhere near them? It's not fair. I come away from wrapping parcels like a seven-stone weakling who's just done 12 rounds with Lennox Lewis. I arrived at the Post Office clutching a few letters and the strangely shaped, sticky, sulking mass that was my barely vanquished parcel, needing to buy stamps and hoping the queue would be short or nonexistent. It wasn't. It was long. I breathed heavily through my nose and joined the end of the line.

Seconds later, two women attached themselves to the queue behind me and began to talk in loud voices about someone at the place where they worked who had earned their disapproval in some way. With considerable relish they swapped anecdotes about how they had *really shown* this unfortunate offender what they thought of her. I listened without appearing to listen, my already dark mood deepening as I listened to such a hymn of unpleasantness. It was then that I gave in to the temptation to play my dreaded 'Post Office Queue Game' for the first time in many years.

When the people in front of me in the queue moved forward a yard or so, I pretended not to notice because I was so absorbed by a notice on the wall. There was a lull in the dialogue behind me. I sensed the minor frustration of these two ladies as they willed me to move into the space that had been created, thus allowing them to move forward as well. I waited until the queue in front of me had progressed yet another pace before appearing to notice for the first time that a gap had opened up. Then I moved on at last – but only about 12 inches. At this, billowing waves of annoyance began to wash over me from behind. Why hadn't I moved right up behind the people in front of me, leaving room for the rest of the queue to do the same? I sensed that a major component of this frustration was the awareness that no logical complaint was justified because we would all be served at exactly the same time, regardless of gaps in the queue.

'But,' they must have been seething and burning to point out to me, 'you *feel* as if you're getting somewhere when you move forward, so why don't you blinking well *move!*'

The discussion about the enemy at work continued, albeit rather disjointedly, but there was no doubt about who had become *numero uno* villain as far as the immediate environment was concerned. I continued to not fill the available gaps in the queue all the way up to the point where it was my turn to be served, preserving throughout an air of innocently detached absent-mindedness which, from time to time, I have found highly successful in deterring open criticism. The two ladies, who happened to end up in the serving position just beside mine, darted little malevolent glances at me as I had my sticky bundle weighed and bought stamps. I smiled at them in an innocently mild, friendly sort of way, and set off home.

It was only as I opened my front gate a few minutes later that I was suddenly filled with shame over my silly game in the Post Office. What right had I to judge the way in which those two people were talking about their workmate? Hadn't I done the same in the past? How could I possibly justify the fact that I had deliberately created anger and frustration in them, just because I was fed up with my messy parcel and my wearying year? I asked Jesus to give me a gift of awareness concerning the things I do to others, things that are so lost in the ordinariness of life that I hardly recognize them as sins, and I asked him to forgive me for being so childish and silly and annoying in the Post Office – and for enjoying it so much.

I follow Jesus because ...
he sometimes lets me visit him in prison

The year of abstinence from public speaking that I mentioned in the last section was a strangely heavy time. Not once did I miss the business of going off to speak to groups of people, much as I enjoy that when I do it, so there was no sense of loss in that area. I suppose it's just that when you stop doing what you do, you tend to discover what you are, and that can be alarming. We very easily talk about the idea that we Christians are nothing and that God is the one who does the business, but it seems to take a lifetime for that piece of knowledge to make the journey from head to heart.

Because of all this, I had rather hoped that my initial re-entry into the world of religious bleating would happen in an environment offering minimum challenge and maximum benefits, but in the event, thank God, I only scored one out of two. Let me explain.

Ever since moving to the town near the south coast where we now live, we have been friendly with a local family made up of two boys, three girls and their mother, June. June is a splendid lady who battled to bring her children up on her own since her husband left in the early years of their marriage. Despite her best efforts, one of the boys, Daniel, got into trouble with the law on many occasions as he was growing up, and as an adult has spent two or three periods in prison, usually for drug-related offences of theft and violence. Despite the fact that Daniel has done some very unpleasant things over the last few years, Bridget and I have always maintained our friendship with him and continued to hope and believe that a change would come about in his life one day.

Just before Christmas on my year off, I was contacted by a man who runs a special project at a prison down in the south-west of England. He explained that he was responsible for a wing that is staffed by Christians and run according to a model that originated in a Brazilian prison where the inmates volunteered to organize themselves because of staff shortages. The unexpected result of this was wide-scale revival in the prison.

Each prisoner who successfully applies to come onto the wing, my caller went on to explain, has to attend a week-end of intensive instruction and discussion on the subject of the Christian faith and its relevance to him as an individual.

The weekend then ends with a service involving all those who have attended, as well as people from outside the prison who provide regular visiting support. This meeting, or 'Closing' as it's known, is normally an occasion of much emotion and shedding of tears, as men face the darkness within them and the light that beckons. Their stay on the wing continues with considerable Christian input from staff and outsiders, together with involvement in a system that is self-regulating and therefore quite demanding on men who are used to surviving in the normal prison ethos.

'Daniel Scott's down here at the moment,' said my caller, having explained all this, 'and he said you'd come down and speak at one of our Monday evening meetings if I asked you.'

And that was why I found myself, one January morning, sitting on a train bound for the West Country, wondering how it was all going to go, and feeling deeply intrigued about Daniel's involvement.

After my five-hour train journey the prison itself turned out to be as depressing as all prisons inevitably are, a grey hulk of a building lowering grimly from the top of a hill across the bay below, but the aggressively dull environment was more than compensated for by the warmth of Daniel's greeting just inside the door of the wing where I was about to speak. To my surprise, there was another old friend of mine with him, a man called Jack whom I had known when, as a boy, he had been admitted into the secure unit where I worked. It was *so good* to be greeted with such enthusiasm.

A little later, though, as I watched 60–70 men troop into the meeting room, my confidence dipped a little. I knew, because I had been told, that not all these men were Christians, and I sensed from the general atmosphere that an easy ride for outside speakers was by no means guaranteed.

I felt quite nervous as I began to speak, but after a few minutes I was overwhelmed by the realization that God wanted to reach out to these people, and I began to relax as I talked simply about the love of God, the heavy demands he makes on our lives and the excitement of wondering exactly how he will use us. Afterwards, I chatted with several of the men, including Daniel and Jack. The change in Daniel was a fascinating one. He seemed almost puzzled by the shift of perspective that he was experiencing.

'The thing is, Adrian,' he said, 'in the past I was so angry, and I tried to solve everything by lashing out, but now – I dunno – there's these new ways of doing things. I really want my life to be different.'

The impression I got from Daniel and other inmates I talked to, as well as from the man who ran the project, was that change in individuals almost invariably begins with encountering the possibility of unconditional love, a love that demands much but will never let go. Nothing has changed much in 2,000 years.

Later, as I was being driven down to the little guesthouse where I was to stay that night, I really thanked God for the privilege of being allowed to be part of what was going on in the prison for just one short evening, and to meet Jesus in the hearts of those men who so wanted their lives to be different. My first engagement of that year had been in the dullest environment you could imagine, with a smaller audience than I was likely to encounter for the whole of the rest of the year, and for the least financial return possible. And yet, I couldn't conceive of a better way for a Christian to begin a busy 12 months of travelling and speaking.

If you have a moment, please say a prayer for Daniel and Jack, and all the others in that wing who are daring to believe that change is possible.

I follow Jesus because ...
among the good things he offers us
is the gift of speaking in tongues

Recent involvement in a debate concerning the gift of 'speaking in tongues' triggered memories of when I first encountered this interesting phenomenon for myself. As a teenager of 16 or 17 in the mid-1960s, I travelled to the town of Sevenoaks every Thursday evening to help at a church-organized event called 'The Cavern' (nothing to do with The Beatles, I'm afraid). Here, a mixture of Christian and non-Christian young people met in a converted cellar under the parish church to drink very weak coffee and listen to very loud music. I had been recently converted, and was determined to pluck as many lost souls from the fires of hell as possible. On reflection, I suspect that I might have repelled many more than I attracted with my hectoring approach to evangelism, but I meant well – I think...

A Christian girl called Marian also came along to The Cavern fairly regularly, and it was from her that I first heard about 'tongues', this strange gift, mentioned in the New Testament in some detail, which apparently enabled those who had received it to speak in languages they had never learned. With the crassness of youth, I asked Marian if she would give some of us a demonstration of her gift and, with great courage, because she was actually a very shy girl, she did. A little circle of us, Christians and non-Christians (the latter even more bewildered than I was, of course), sat in a back room and waited expectantly for the 'magic' to begin. Marian asked the Holy Spirit to help her, and then started to speak softly in something that certainly sounded to my ears like a completely different language.

I don't know how anyone else reacted to what they heard on that winter evening in Sevenoaks, but I was fascinated and deeply excited. It was my first real intimation that God could be present in the lives of his followers in a much more immediate way than I had ever imagined. On investigating (that means I read about it) the scriptural basis for such things, I was even more enthralled to discover that 'tongues' appeared to be the *least* of the gifts, and that we were exhorted by Paul to ask even more earnestly for the gift of prophecy, which would be vitally useful to the whole body of the church. I started to visit a local Pentecostal church in the mornings, as well as continuing to attend Evensong at my usual Anglican church, so that I could see gifts being used in the services.

In the course of the next year I started to speak in tongues myself, although, try as I might, I cannot recall a specific moment when this began. I found and still find this gift richly valuable in my private prayer, as it seems to excavate love and longing from the depths of my psyche, but – let me be absolutely honest with you – for a long time I felt a tinge of doubt about the whole business. Was my tongue really a tongue, or was I kidding myself? Was it just a meaningless babble that made me feel a bit better?

Then, one Tuesday evening, four or five years ago, something happened. The Bible study group which Bridget and I were leading at the time had been listening to a visiting speaker who had come with his wife. After the talk, which was excellent, a member of the group asked about the gift of tongues, and was prayed for by our visitor with no immediately apparent result.

I was feeling very uneasy. I had almost never spoken in tongues in front of anyone before and, unlike my old friend Marian, I didn't have the courage to volunteer a demonstration now, good idea though it might well have been. As soon as I could decently do it, I began one of those comfortable mopping-up prayers that always precede the coffee and biscuits. Imagine my horror when the prayer that I had begun in English moved seamlessly into being the most fluent tongue that I had ever heard coming out of my own mouth. When I finished, our visiting speaker's wife interpreted the message (interpretation being another distinct gift, of course), although I registered nothing of what she said, and I had to sit down as I was feeling rather shaky. You just can't trust God at all, can you?

I greatly value these experiences, but I would like to be absolutely clear about where I stand on this matter. Many, if not most, followers of Jesus have never spoken and will never speak in tongues. The Bible teaches that this, the least of the gifts, is not in any sense an essential part of Christian experience, whatever some misguided teachers might suggest.

Having said that, why shouldn't we ask Jesus to give us as many gifts as will be useful to us and to the churches where we worship? Whether it's tongues or teaching, hospitality or healing, each one is valuable, and God is a generous giver to those who are ready to gratefully receive.

I follow Jesus because ...
he truly understands what being part of a human family means

There was one week last year when two apparently unconnected but significant events occurred. The first was the birth of Thomas Patrick McCusker, and the second was the departure of the priest in charge of our church.

A few years ago I collaborated on a book with Paul McCusker, an experienced American writer who has been extremely successful in the United States in the field of radio drama. Our jointly written book, *You Say Tomato*, is a collection of fictional letters exchanged by George, an Englishman, and Brad, an American. We wrote the book in three weeks, sitting at our individual word processors in a rented cottage near Hailsham, finding the process stressful, combative and fascinating. The result, published in 1995, was greeted in America and England with resounding puzzlement, positive appreciation and silence. Paul can't have found this unusual experience too negative, because later he and his wife Elizabeth moved to England, where they now live in the same town as us.

Thomas Patrick, their first-born, arrived at half past eight one Friday evening, and we first saw him on the following day.

There is, of course, an important ritual to be observed with new babies. First, you ask about the birth weight. If it was more than eight pounds you utter a gasp of approval. If the little scrap was at the lower end of the scale you sigh fondly. Thomas Patrick emerged weighing six pounds six ounces, a weight which leaves one rather dumb. Bridget and I still felt vaguely obligated to respond rapturously, but it would have sounded odd to say with enormous enthusiasm, 'Gosh! Six pounds six ounces! That's – that's really, amazingly average, isn't it? Wow!'

Fortunately, Tommy himself was enough to produce genuine rapture. We're suckers for babies, and this one, besides being nothing more than an alimentary canal in a bag, like all babies, was beautiful. The sight of him triggered part two of the ritual. Which parent did he most resemble, and which features provided the clues? No room for debate there. If a fierce, head-shrinking South American tribe had blow-piped Paul in the Amazon forest one day, removed his head, taken it back to camp and reduced it to a third of its original size, the face on it would have been exactly the same as Tommy's. That baby was the image of his father. You could see it in the eyes, the mouth, and – to be noted with gentle sadness – the ears.

What has this to do with our minister moving on?

At a party held for the aforesaid minister and his family a couple of days later, we discussed which of Jeremy's many qualities as a priest had been most appreciated. The one that sprang to my mind was his habit of producing little nuggets of original thought in sermons, nuggets that I always tucked away at the back of my mind for possible use in my writing. Often these little gems were throw-away comments, things that we shameless, vulture-like scribblers leap upon and consume with hasty relish.

On this farewell evening, probably because of Tommy, I remembered Jeremy saying that, as well as having the spiritual characteristics of his heavenly Father, Jesus must also have inherited physical features from Mary, his mother. This self-evident fact had never occurred to me and after rolling it around my mind I stored it away, filed in my imagination, as it were, under 'Nose'.

Thinking about Tommy and Mary and Jesus provoked one of those chewy questions that are exciting because they force me into producing an answer, or at least a guess, in the form of poetry, story or drama.

When Mary first saw the resurrected Jesus, did she consciously or unconsciously check that the little parts of him inherited from her were still intact? We shall never know on this side of the grave, of course. One day we can ask Mary herself, but, in the meantime, isn't it interesting to conjecture?

Those real-life, legendary, famous men
Who ate the Sabbath corn with him a thousand
*   puzzled memories ago*
Are far more confident today

They play their humble trumpets in the market place
Clarion the truth
How Jesus was and is the image of his Father
Full of love and grace and truth
And yes, of course – of course he was and is his
    Father's son
The Holy One, the Saviour
Yes, of course
And yet, you know, that baby, once so closely mine
That baby who became a boy, a man, and much,
    much more
Inherited from me the things my mother's heart loved
    best
His nose
His ears
That way he had of lifting up his chin when the road
    was getting rough
Such special joy to see those sweet, sweet things all
    risen with the rest
Not much perhaps, but privately, for me – enough.

I wonder what Jesus and his mum talk about nowadays.

I follow Jesus because ...
he's kinder and more merciful than those
who have done dreadful things in his name
during the last 2,000 years

I started to cry as I watched the television one night. This
sudden descent into tears was not because the quality of
the programme that happened to be on at the time was so
poor, but rather because the events depicted in this particular episode of *Cadfael* made me remember, with a sudden

overwhelming rush of feeling, how deeply attracted I am by the mercy and kindness of God.

Cadfael, a fictional but beautifully drawn character created by the writer Ellis Peters, is a highly intelligent, sensitive monk who specializes in solving mediaeval murder mysteries. As you probably know, the *Cadfael* books are immensely popular, as is the television series of the same name starring Derek Jacobi, for my money one of the finest stage and screen actors of his generation.

In the episode that affected me so much, Cadfael was investigating two deaths, one that of a rather satisfyingly growly and unpleasant monk who had recently arrived to take up the position of Prior at the monastery in which the story was set, and the other a single girl who had become pregnant by an unknown man. This young girl had approached the new Prior seeking confession and absolution for her sin, but had been cruelly repulsed and branded an evil woman. All the evidence available to Cadfael suggested that, in response to this rejection, she had committed lonely suicide by casting herself into a millstream that ran behind the Priory.

At the point of history in which *Cadfael* is set, suicide was regarded by the church as a mortal sin. Those who successfully sought such a cataclysmic escape from their problems were invariably buried in unconsecrated ground and reckoned to have certainly forfeited their salvation. Cadfael's hope was that by discovering she had in fact been murdered, he might ensure that her body would receive Christian burial.

Now, I'm afraid that's about as much of the storyline as I can share with you, not because I'm worried about spoiling it for you if you see it one day, but simply because I have never in my life understood more than about a tenth of what's going on in *any* whodunit that I have ever read or watched. I enjoy them, you understand, but my brain is simply not up to following the twists and turns of the plot. Even when I watch *Columbo*, perhaps my favourite detective series of all, where in every single episode you *know* who did it from the very start, I'm in a complete fog from beginning to end.

From out of the fog on this *Cadfael* occasion came two things that made me tearful.

The first was a moment when another monk from the monastery declared loudly that the pregnant girl had been nothing but a useless whore, and Cadfael said with a mixture of quiet indignation and sorrow, almost to himself, 'She wasn't a whore, she was a child.'

The second was an incident at the very end of the episode, after it had been clearly proved that the young expectant mother had indeed taken her own life, as had originally been assumed. Going out secretly to the place where her body lay in unconsecrated ground, Cadfael buried a little crucifix on a chain in the freshly turned earth of her grave.

Tears filled my eyes. Perhaps you will think me foolish, but I don't really care. Those two moments reminded me with an extraordinary power and abruptness that the God whom we try to serve is far more compassionate than most of his followers, let alone his opponents. We all fall woefully short of the ideal, and we thank God for Jesus who forgives sin and binds up the brokenhearted and understands and allows us to begin again.

In a very different work, *Three Men in a Boat*, written around the turn of the century, Jerome K. Jerome describes how he and his friends discover a young woman's corpse in the river, and learn later that, having given birth out of wedlock, she became so oppressed by poverty and loneliness that she ended her own life.

'She had sinned,' says Jerome. 'Some of us do that now and then, you know...'

Well, yes, we jolly well do, and most of us know well enough what we've done without having our noses rubbed in it by the sort of tight-lipped harbingers of doom who have hurt so many Christians who were already hurting more than they could imagine. Thank God Jesus is in charge.

As I watched *Cadfael* I found myself thanking God that all through history there have been people who, often against the spirit of the age or the spiritual fashion, really are inhabited by the sweet Spirit of Jesus, that Spirit who never compromises, but is always ready to forgive and embrace those who have been cast out by men but are still able to turn to him. Thank God for those people who keep alive the essential truth that God is wise and warm and sane and adult and understanding and forgiving and full of divine common sense, because they are the people who show the Saviour to the world.

Don't laugh. I know it was only a fictional programme, but God created television as well as everything else, and on that particular evening, he used it.

I follow Jesus because ...
he values everyone equally and is
teaching me to do the same

This is the story of how a journey into the past affected the present.

My father-in-law, who has lived in Norwich since before Bridget was born, celebrated his ninetieth birthday by spending a week in the beautiful county of Lancashire where he was born and raised in the early part of this century. My wife's brother and sister-in-law and their two children joined the whole of our family for this significant event, the mark of a long life which, in its own way, is a powerful advertisement for moderation.

Bridget's father, George Ormerod, who was employed as a clerk in one of our major High Street banks for the whole of his working life, has been quite immoderately committed to moderation for the whole of his 90 years, and therefore leads a more exciting life than anybody else I know. This is bound to be so when *everything* unexpected is an adventure. On those rare occasions, for instance, when an unscheduled visitor knocks on the door of the Ormerod home in Norwich, life moves swiftly into *Raiders of the Lost Ark* mode as George half-rises worriedly from the chair in which he always sits, nervously conjecturing about who could possibly be disturbing the pattern of his normal life in such a dramatic fashion.

He has eaten exactly the same healthy combination of things at breakfast-time for as long as anyone who knows him can remember, chewing each mouthful of food the same number of times, exactly as he was instructed to do as a boy, and he never eats between meals, except at Christmas, when a discreet sweet and a very small glass from the bottle of liqueur that has already lasted for three years are entirely permissible, because they are tiny but unvarying details in the overall moderate pattern.

Over the years George has enjoyed visits from his son and daughter and their families, although the healthily anarchic tendencies of our respective children have disturbed and confused him from time to time. One of the most fascinating aspects of George's fanatical drive to avoid excess has been his quite amazing ability simply to avoid seeing those things that blatantly deny his perception of his own attitudes and habits. Sometimes, for example, the children will turn the television on in Nanna and Grandpa's house and a situation comedy will be announced.

'Oh,' says Grandpa uneasily, as the opening music is heard and the titles appear, 'we never watch this. We don't find it funny.'

Throughout the programme (which Nanna insists on allowing because the children enjoy it), George guffaws and chortles with laughter at the jokes, clearly enjoying every minute. As the credits come up at the end, however, he shakes his head and announces once again to the world at large, without any trace of self-consciousness, 'We never watch that programme, you know. We don't find it funny.'

One of the major benefits of this very regular way of life, apart from the constant excitement, of course, is that George is extremely fit for a man of his age. A little more wheezy than in the past, perhaps, but still able to enjoy not only regular swimming sessions at a local pool, but also those evenly paced walks that have been a favourite habit since he first met his wife on a walking holiday in the Lake District before the war. For nine decades, George has been going 'steadily on', as he puts it, and, at the time of writing, there's no visible reason why he shouldn't go 'steadily on' for another 10 years and reach the century that, as an ex-cricketer, would greatly appeal to him.

Relations between my father-in-law and I were, you won't be surprised to hear, more than a little strained when we first met. I was about as far from being moderate as it's possible to be. Poor George must have felt that his only daughter was being swept up into some kind of emotional and social 'twister' that would inevitably leave her damaged and disappointed. It took many years for him to understand and accept that Bridget has a tendency towards doing a spot of twisting of her own, and that we have always hung onto each other in the centre of the storm.

I have had to do some understanding and accepting as well. As a child of the '60s, I wore contempt for what I thought of as the stuffy old previous generation like a cheap badge. I was unthinkingly intolerant and scornful of those who appeared reluctant to explore extremities of experience in the way that 'free spirits' like me were prepared to do. What did a career matter? What did money matter? What did the future matter? Why should we be concerned about such trivial issues? Those were the sorts of intelligent thing that I was saying. George must have been utterly bewildered by me and my unexpected intrusion into his family. As far as my future father-in-law was concerned, an alien had landed and communication was a problem, to say the least. Now, I can understand why it was so difficult for him, and trips like the one we made to Clitheroe, his home town, have deepened that understanding.

The part of northern England where George grew up was cotton country, a region where hundreds of mills turned out cotton for markets all over the world. In those days it would have been reckoned more or less inevitable that George should go into that same trade, just as many members of his family had done before him. Instead, young George Ormerod, a mild, undemonstrative lad with a rather attractive blue-eyed smile, brought up in a house where the atmosphere was permanently hushed because of his mother's chronic illness, and with a record of considerable academic ability at school, managed to secure a job at the bank in Blackburn at the age of 15. At that time, and in that part of the world, this was a considerable achievement. It was a breaking away from what was expected, an opportunity to move upwards and onwards, a chance for George to really build a future for himself. Nowadays, it doesn't seem like much, but then, in the early 1920s, it was quite something. George was a child of the '20s.

While we were in Clitheroe on this occasion we drove past the small, stone-built house where George was brought up, and parked beside the cricket pitch on the other side of the road, where, in the recently modernized pavilion, we found an old black-and-white photograph of the Clitheroe cricket team of 74 years ago. The picture showed not only the 11 members of the team, but also the scorer, G. T. Ormerod, 15 years old, smiling nervously but proudly at the camera from his humble position behind the heroes of the side.

George went on to play for and captain one of the Clitheroe teams, and he also became superintendent of the children's Sunday School at his church, a massive responsibility in those days, when large numbers of children attended every week. All in all he was an involved and integrated member of his community, a person who did things and went to things and belonged.

I don't suppose George and I would ever have been soulmates exactly, but my early negative feelings have given way to a realization that his humanity is, in the context of his own growing-up and development, as rich with the stuff of life as anyone else's, including mine. I trust that he has adjusted his view of me as well.

May Jesus help us all to avoid falling into the trap of believing that any other person is automatically worth less than us because the way they are, or the way they have lived, is beyond our understanding and experience. We shall all be making the same journey home in the end, so we might as well start learning to understand and appreciate each other now.

I follow Jesus because ...
he's not meteorologically selective

Do you have faith in the weather forecast? Agnostic? Nonbeliever? Recent convert? Follower of the great prophet Fish?

Believe it or not, but I have detected a most interesting link between the way in which television weather forecasts are delivered in this country and the problems that many Christians have with understanding the place of suffering in their lives. Now, don't flick on to the next section. I know it's an unlikely connection, but read on.

First, let's just reflect on how this sort of programme has altered over the last few years. There was a time when weather forecasts had a narrowly defined function – namely, to forecast the weather. Crudely simple, eh? A smartly respectable, inexpensively suited gentleman with a vaguely scientific air would apologetically suggest the kind of weather we might possibly experience during the next 24 hours. Having delivered his faltering prediction, this prophetic rabbit would dive back into the meteorological burrow from which he had emerged, and not reappear until another forecast was due. He was never right, of course, but that in itself was most helpful when planning activities. If the expert proclaimed that the weekend was going to be cold and wet, we dug out the suntan oil and headed for the beach. If he said it was going to be warm and sunny, we ordered in an extra load of coal and got angry because someone had pinched the dice from the Monopoly set.

Nowadays, weather forecasts bristle with high-tech gadgets and snappy little cartoon-like symbols, and are almost always delivered by young, beautiful people who wouldn't know a warm front from a deep depression, but see pop-meteorology as a handy backdoor entrance to fame and fortune. Indeed, one or two of these incredibly white-toothed, professionally engaging men and women have actually gone on to minor stardom in isobar-free areas of entertainment.

One consequence of this changed style has been a tendency on the part of the forecasters to inject personal bias into what they say. Thus we have acquired a whole new set of values for each type of weather, largely based on the way in which Bright Young Things tend to see the world.

Rain, for instance, is always bad, despite the fact that, for excellent and obvious reasons, it's actually very good. 'Bad news, I'm afraid. We're in for a few showers,' says a Bright Young Thing sadly, dismissing our forthcoming copious supplies of a substance that some people value beyond gold. Bright Young Things have no use for rain. Call me weird, but I'm so glad that we get lots of rain, and I *love* walking in it.

Sunshine is always, always good. 'I'm pleased to say that I can promise you some sunshine!' trills the B.Y.T. chirpily. I agree that sunshine is very often good, but an unrelieved diet of sunny days would bore me stiff. Like Chesterton, I can enjoy all weather except what the English call a 'Glorious Day'.

Snow is always bad if it stops you getting to the wine bar from the studio, but it's allowed to be good if it falls in places where the Bright Young Things are hoping to ski at the weekend.

And so on, and so on. Day by day, bit by bit, a whole generation of telly-watching kids has been taught to celebrate the sun and rage against the rain.

Now, leaving aside your growing and ludicrous conviction that I'm actually talking about my own resentment at being dull and middle-aged instead of bright and young, there's a parallel here with the kind of teaching on suffering that the church has mistakenly offered over the last 20 years. Perhaps because we Western Christians are always trying – albeit unconsciously – to justify the luxury of our lifestyle, there has been a tendency to teach that the rain of suffering is a sign of spiritual weakness or inadequacy, whereas the sunshine of health and prosperity is an indication that God is smiling on us.

I regard this as dangerous nonsense.

A cursory reading of the Gospels makes it plain that this isn't the case at all. Jesus clearly warned his disciples to expect some very tough times indeed. 'If you think I've had it difficult, wait until you see what happens to you,' might be a rough but fairly accurate paraphrase of his words to that little band of followers, who really hadn't the faintest idea what he was talking about at the time. Later, they knew.

I don't mean that we have to like bad things happening to us. Jesus wasn't a loony and he doesn't expect us to be either, but our very right to go home to God was bought with the most significant act of suffering in the history of our planet. I don't think we should despise our suffering. I think we should offer our pain to God and tell him to do what he likes with it. We may be amazed.

Having said all that, what really happens when the crunch comes and we're right in the middle of genuine agony? The book of James instructs us to regard all trials and difficulties as pure joy. Help! What sense does that make in the real world?

This stark question takes me back to a time when I had cracked or broken one of my ribs. Stepping into the shower one day, I slipped on the bottom of the bath and fell backwards, hitting the right side of my upper back on the rim of the bath with a sickening crunch. Those who have seen me in the flesh (evil word!) will know just what a crunch that must have been. Remembering that injunction from jolly old James, I obediently sang a bright little chorus of appreciation as I was in the act of falling, and celebrated the impact itself with a loud 'whoop!' of pure joy.

The whole of the previous sentence is, I humbly confess, totally and outrageously untrue – but isn't it interesting how many things do go through one's mind during that short, dramatic, involuntary journey from the vertical to the horizontal? In an oddly dispassionate, detached sort of way, I recall finding myself thinking about the implications of the fall – mine I mean, not the one that has slightly more profound theological implications – even as I descended. Would I be injured so badly, I wondered, that Bridget would have to get help to remove my naked body from the bathroom? Please, God, let it *not* be so. Would it be necessary to go down to the accident and emergency department of our local hospital? If so, would they admit me for a night or more, and how many of my engagements would be affected as a consequence? Might I be so seriously hurt that my general mobility would be reduced for the rest of my life? Had I damaged the bath? By the time I actually hit the side of the bath I seemed to have thought the whole thing through quite thoroughly. It hardly seemed worth the bother of actually landing.

As it happened, I was immobilized to the extent that I had to cancel a whole month of speaking appointments, and, as day after day of stillness passed, I developed a deep sympathy for those whose pain is chronic and incurable. Inevitably I was also drawn once more into this consideration of the meaning and significance of suffering in the lives of Christians, not least because I had a very particular and accessible case to study – my own. I had always adhered to the view that suffering is by no means an exclusively negative experience for those who wish to follow Jesus. To what extent was that really true in my own immediate circumstances? Did the 'pure joy' principle mean anything at all? I examined the evidence.

First of all, there was the fact that, to all intents and purposes, I was anchored to one end of the sofa that stood against the wall in our sitting room. One corner of this specific piece of furniture was, for reasons that I didn't quite understand, the only place in the house where I was able to experience reasonable comfort for the first week or two of my injury. Since I was unable to lie down at all, that same corner was also the place where I slept at night in a sitting position, but only for smallish chunks of time. Occasionally, when I was awake, I used my remote control device to surf through the endless Sky channels on television, seeking company from flickering screen images through the long watches of the night. In the early hours of the morning I was sometimes confronted by wild-eyed, ranting evangelists. I owe a great debt to these men. The therapy they offered was immensely effective. Emotions of anger reminded me that I was still alive and reacting to things, a very good thing for one who is obliged to remain virtually motionless.

Was this enforced anchorage a negative aspect of what happened to me? Well, yes, but not as far as my 10-year-old daughter was concerned. Katy just *loved* having her daddy pinned down to one near-permanent spot. She knew exactly where I was at any given point during the night or day. When she went to bed, there I was on the end of the sofa. When she got up and came down in the morning, there I was on the end of the sofa. She set off for school leaving me on the sofa; she returned to find me in exactly the same place. I became a sort of 'pet daddy', a large, uncaged hamster, always available to cuddle, or talk to, or ask for money. She really enjoyed it and so, I must admit, did I. Perhaps I should have realized long before then how positively my children would benefit from seeing me sit still for a while.

Then there was the fact that I was unable to do any work that involved travelling. At first that certainly seemed a 100 per cent, definite, cast-iron, indisputable negative, but after a couple of weeks I wasn't so sure. In the fortnight following my last meeting before getting crocked I received so many visitors who really only needed the ear of someone who had enough time on his hands to hear them out. These people most decidedly did not come because they knew I was stranded at home for a while. Rather, it was as if some kind of vacuum had been created by my inactivity, allowing those with troubled hearts to flow in and fill the space. Most importantly, perhaps, very close friends who lived nearby and had hit a very rough patch in their lives at this particular time desperately needed help and support in carrying their burdens. I thank God that, inadequate as I was, I was able to be there for them. Positive wins again.

What about sheer physical discomfort? Am I about to claim that excruciating pain proved, against all reasonable expectations, to be really rather jolly? No, I make no such claim, for the simple reason that it wasn't the case. The pain was awful, and would have been worse if it hadn't been for the use of powerful painkillers prescribed by my doctor. (You may be interested to learn, by the way, that the label on the bottle containing these tablets conveyed a stern warning that drowsiness might occur, and that it would therefore be unwise for me to operate agricultural machinery. Can you begin to picture the inner battles I fought and won to resist my natural inclination to operate agricultural machinery at every opportunity?) No, the pain was horrible, but, as I have already mentioned, my sympathy for folk who are never likely to see an end to their suffering deepened with every day that brought me nearer to relief and healing. I thank God for that as well.

Speaking of God – did he do it? Did God, out of the goodness of his heart, hide in the bathroom and pop out to give me a little shove as I was about to step into the shower, knowing that all the aforementioned subtle benefits would accrue to me if I broke a rib? Or might it conceivably have been the devil who did the shoving, hoping to drive me into a position where, just as he had vainly hoped with Job, I would wail and complain about the unfair way in which my creator had used me? Or could it possibly be that the absence of an anti-slip mat on the bottom of the bath, an omission I should have rectified ages ago, was the main reason for my accident? I don't pretend to know the final answers to such questions, but I must confess that the last one, deeply mystical as it is, seems the most likely to me.

Whatever the truth may be, I'm sure of one thing – and herein lies the 'pure joy' that really might underlie and contain all misfortunes – I'm sure that God is in charge and that he loves us. Whether he causes situations of this kind, or whether he simply uses them, we can be certain that, in the most important sense, we're perfectly safe.

Just occasionally, you know, even as I sat nursing my injury, the knowledge of his caring parenthood made me want to laugh out loud. I didn't give in to the temptation because it would have made my ribs hurt.

I follow Jesus because ...
he brings something good out of the
most (apparently) awful events

Early one morning that phone of mine rang. I have very mixed feelings about the sound of a ringing telephone, don't you? When I'm expecting good news it's a sweet, hopeful sound, whereas, when it rings in the middle of the night, when no one should be calling anyone else, my heart sinks in anticipation of some terrible information flying into my life like a missile to destroy sleep and peace. Or it might be an Australian. The rest of the time – well, I suppose that shrill call to communication is a neutral sound, until you pick up the receiver, that is.

The ring I'm talking about was from a man calling to say that a friend of ours had died in the early hours of the morning after a fall in her house the day before. My wife and I knew that Shelagh had been injured, but, as far as we were aware, she had simply banged her head after tripping on the stairs, and we assumed that she would recover after appropriate treatment. After all, we had seen her only a few days ago, and she was as right as rain. I now learned that this fall down the stairs had caused internal bleeding, which, despite an emergency operation, ultimately proved to be fatal.

How silly and trivial the causes of death appear some-times. Somebody knocks on your front door, you hurry to the stairs to go down and let them in, your foot slips on the carpet, you fall awkwardly and suddenly the whole thing is over. No more questions, no more conversations, no more prayer, no more sips of wine, no more love or anger or tiredness or elation – not in this world, at any rate. How was it possible for someone who had been so whole and complex and human to be gone so completely? There are no degrees of death, are there? You can't be fairly dead, or very dead indeed, or less dead in comparison with someone else. You're just dead, and there's an end of it.

Shelagh, a single lady, was a Christian, a firm believer in the living Jesus – he who just that morning had received her with great joy even as we were releasing her from the landscape of our minds with such sorrow. She was a priest in the Anglican church, a writer of some accomplishment, and the editor of *New Daylight*, a booklet of daily Bible notes published by the Bible Reading Fellowship, which appears at four-monthly intervals and is read all over the world. Each edition features contributions from several writers, of whom I'm privileged to be one.

Some editors of Bible note collections are almost destructively censorious towards the work of their contributors. One well-known writer who's involved with a different publisher told my wife the other day that she had to search carefully through the printed sections that bore her name to find some trace of the pieces that she had originally written. This wasn't Shelagh's style at all. She was insistent that the very varied personalities of her team members should be allowed to give flavour and interest to the notes they wrote, so that, like the prophets of the Old Testament (I should be so lucky!), each one might emphasize a different facet or attribute of the nature of God. Shelagh's view appeared to be, 'If God isn't ashamed to be closely associated with Adrian Plass, then neither am I.'

It will take me a long time to get used to the fact that Shelagh is no longer with us, and a lot of people will miss her very much.

So, what is it possible for the Holy Spirit to teach us from what many regarded as the untimely death of this individual Christian person? Well, let me begin by saying that I meet quite a lot of vicars and church leaders who have lost heart or become worried because congregations are not as co-operative as they were, because there seems far too much work to do for one man or woman, and because the changing, evolving world threatens to overtake and engulf their role in society. I think the problem is a universal one, but let's not lose heart.

Here are some things that, through the death of Shelagh, have been brought into my mind.

First, the human being to whom she owes the greatest debt of all is that person who led her to a belief in Jesus many years ago. When the chips are down (an old theological expression), all that matters is the future of our eternal souls. We don't want to die the second death, as it's called in the book of Revelation, and it's because of vicars and church leaders all over the world that people like Shelagh walk straight into the arms of Jesus when their mortal bodies cease to function. They will live for ever because they belong to him. Church leaders shouldn't despise or lose sight of their high calling as harvesters for the Lord. The world is never going to evolve into a place where eternal life is no longer an issue. They are the guardians of this knowledge. They should be proud in the best sense, and pray for chances to lead others to the one who feels such compassion for those who live in ignorance.

Secondly, I think of Shelagh's passion for the personality of God to be expressed in different ways through the variety of people who wrote for *New Daylight*. God isn't calling leaders to produce a group of people who are all exactly the same. They're agents of divine freedom, that freedom which allows followers of Jesus to be extravagantly authentic versions of themselves. God isn't interested in religious conformity, or safe and stolid Christianity. He wants followers who will dive into the deep water of faith like babies who have never had drowning explained to them. There's nothing wrong with allowing folk to thrash about and make mistakes as they learn to swim. Rather, we should celebrate the profound truth expressed in the thirty-second verse of the eighth chapter of the Gospel of John and pass it on with joy to our congregations, praying that they will be submissive to Christ only.

Thirdly, I think of Shelagh's openness to advice and guidance from others. Is it possible, dear one-man-band ministers, for you to become just a little more vulnerable to those whom you serve? When I first began to speak to groups of Christians, I assumed it was essential for me to keep my problems entirely to myself, so that God would be given a 'good reference' whenever I spoke about him. Then, one day, when I was supposed to be delivering a talk on parenting, I confessed that I had been shouting at my children for 24 hours and that my wife and I were not speaking because of an argument on the way to the conference. I thought the audience would walk out in disgust, but the opposite happened. They were released to talk about their own family problems, which was, of course, the reason they had come to the seminar in the first place. There's something very intimidating about being addressed by perfect beings. If you're weary and failing because you feel unsupported, try telling people. It may be embarrassing, but it may also change your ministry.

Finally, my dear fellow lovers of Jesus who aren't ministers, can we try to be gentle with those who carry the burden of being signposts to heaven for us? There are no sinless human beings remaining since Jesus returned to his Father, and church leaders have no special dispensation in this area. In fact, the Bible tells us that they are to be judged more strictly than others because theirs is such a great responsibility. If somebody in our church offers us a criticism of the minister, how about resolving to answer it with a positive comment? We certainly won't be thanked for ruining the 'gossip game', but we will at least have supported the person who, contrary to what many worshippers think, is often the most easily hurt member of the congregation.

My friend has gone to be with Jesus, but we must continue with the work that we're doing here. May the inspiration of those who have, like Shelagh, done their best and departed to Paradise sustain and strengthen us in our resolve to seek the kingdom of God above all things, both for ourselves and for others.

I follow Jesus because ...
I don't want to get stuck or left behind in someone else's camp

Do you belong to a Christian camp? Keep that question in the back of your mind while I ask you another. What do you like doing best?

One of my favourite activities in all the world is to be with other Christians (preferably ones who are unlikely to start spraying condemnation or ministry around too freely), just nattering and gossiping about God. The wonderful thing about such encounters, whether they happen in a church or a pub or a car or a walk in the country or around a kitchen table, is that they become a kind of prayer in themselves. It's strange and significant, isn't it, that some of the most profoundly spiritual moments of our lives tend to be dismissed as merely secular events. It has taken me most of my 51 years on earth to understand that God finds arthritically religious activities as abominable as I do – almost certainly more so.

I remember, for instance, an evening when three of us

met at a friend's house to eat a supper of bread and cheese and wine, and to engage in exactly the kind of nattering and gossiping that I have already mentioned. These two friends of mine are elders in a lively church in the local sea-side town of Eastbourne, one that my family and I don't attend. We know each other very well, though, having met socially on as regular a basis as possible for the last 11 or 12 years. In the course of those many meetings we must have discussed everything under the sun, including just about every aspect of the faith we share. Nevertheless, because of the way the Holy Spirit is, and because of the way good friends are, there's always something new to talk about, especially when there are no silly restrictions on subject matter, and no negative kneejerk reactions to unpalatable truths.

The occasion in question was a little different. All three of us had been nursing a growing feeling that we would like our meetings to have a slightly more specifically religious seal set upon them, but none of us quite knew how this should be done. James, who was our host on this occasion, suggested that we should hold a little private Communion at the beginning or end of each meeting, and at first this seemed a very good idea. A few minutes of structure and formality would just about fit the bill, we reckoned, lending, as such an arrangement surely must, a reassuringly spiritual authenticity to our gatherings.

I can't tell you how glad I was that we abandoned this idea in the end. Almost simultaneously the three of us realized that our motivation for seeking ceremony and form was based much more on fear and the need for a feeling of worldly security than on any spiritual instinct. The desire and drive within human beings to make camp, to build a home, to establish a base, is so strong that it can easily be mistaken for Christian common sense, and end up ruining a

God-given situation in which we have found ourselves riskily, excitingly, disturbingly, usefully free. The itch that James and Ben and I had actually been attempting to scratch was a vague feeling that, if we weren't some kind of recognizable *churchy thing*, we didn't really exist in the eyes of God.

I would hate you to misunderstand me. I love the Communion service. It's part of my joy and my duty and my life. Similarly, I love the church in Hailsham of which I'm a member. I want and need to belong to it. A church doesn't have to be a camp. But if, at some point in the future, those activities and that community were to stop being a caravan and become a settlement, I might have to move on, because I want to follow Jesus, and I feel a new gratitude that God has given me my two friends to accompany me on these very special occasions as I trudge along behind him.

This issue was highlighted for me a few days later when I met a man (let's call him Derek) who for some years had been an important figure in one of the largest and best known church communities in Great Britain. He described to me his feelings when, after being one of the founder members of the church and serving as an elder during the crucial years of its development, he found himself 'side-lined' for reasons that were as flimsy as they were cruel.

'To be honest, Adrian,' he said, 'I feel as if I've been dumped outside the camp, and that's a very lonely place to be.'

'There is no camp, Derek,' I said, 'and if there is, I offer you my congratulations on getting out of it. Jesus still walks the road ahead of us, just as he led his disciples 2,000 years ago, and we're still called to trudge along behind him, talking nonsense and doing what we're told, just as they did. If some people want to stop following him and make a nice tidy camp by the roadside – well, that's their business. We must walk on, because we never were supposed to have anywhere to lay our heads, and we won't have, not this side of heaven. I understand how hurt you feel, but I reckon you're in the right place.'

After that, I'm glad to say, there seemed to be a new spring in Derek's spiritual step.

As for James and Ben and me, well, we have agreed that our meetings will now begin with a prayer in which we offer *everything* that's said and done and eaten and drunk and thought to God. Apart from that, though, nothing will alter our regular trudge unless the suggestion for change comes from the Holy Spirit. Our most fervent prayer as the years go by is that our feet will hold out, our ears will stay tuned, and we will continue excitedly to follow the truth.

I follow Jesus because ...
he doesn't ask me to adapt as much as Saint John of the Cross would have had to if he'd been booked to address the West Fittlewick Over-Sixties Interdenominational Ladies' Afternoon Club at three o'clock on a wet Thursday afternoon in November

Would it surprise you to learn that, every now and then, I complain about certain aspects of my life? No, I didn't think it would. I've been much too honest in this book. I sense that the stage of being seen as endearingly vulnerable has passed. You just expect the worst now, don't you? Oh well, never mind...

Yes, sometimes I do complain, and recently my complaints have been about the extraordinary degree of on-the-spot adaptation required for various speaking engagements.

When I'm not feeling tired or sad, I actively enjoy the process of selecting the next piece of material even as I'm in the middle of delivering the present one, but it can be very hard going at other times.

In this connection I do have to confess that at first a little resentment crept in when I thought about spiritual communicators of the past. How would they have coped? Take Saint John of the Cross, for instance. A great thinker, writer and man of God, naturally, but if he had ever made the foolish mistake of getting himself booked to address the West Fittlewick Over-Sixties Interdenominational Ladies' Afternoon Club at three o'clock on a wet Thursday afternoon in November, might he not have given up mysticism altogether and run away to join the circus? I think he would, don't you?

I mean, just allow your imagination to picture the scene for a moment. A grave, bearded figure, dressed in the monk-like costume of his own era, gets off the bus just outside West Fittlewick village hall and arrives 15 minutes early, as arranged, to be greeted at the door by Mrs Stamford-Jones, the club president. Ushering him through the porch and into the body of the hall, she whispers with chatty confidentiality in his left ear.

'Word to the wise, Saint John – may I call you Saint John, or do you prefer Mr Cross? – some of our more elderly ladies will more than likely drop off after about 10 minutes, or start needing the – you know – the facilities, so if you could speak up nice and loud and cheerful and keep it to no more than about 15 minutes, that would be lovely. And then we all have tea. To be quite honest,' she giggles a little, 'our ladies really look forward to that more than anything. And we've allocated a nice piece of cake for you, so don't worry.'

Several minutes after this inspirational first encounter, it's time for the public introduction. Mrs Stamford-Jones rises to her feet and clears her throat. Saint John of the Cross, strangely unreassured by the fact that a nice piece of cake has been allocated to him, shifts wretchedly and uneasily on an orange plastic chair, his thoughts already straying to the attractive prospect of high-trapeze work or lion-taming.

'Right, ladies, let's make a start, shall we? *Nice* to see so many of you here today – nearly 20 at a quick count – and we do hope those of you who've come for the first time will have a really lovely afternoon and want to come again. Now – last month Mr Simmonds came with his projector to give us slides of West Fittlewick As It Was, and as usual a wonderful time was had by all, as I'm sure we'd all agree, wouldn't we?' Invitational pause. Murmurs and clucks of agreement from the ladies. 'Now, this month we are extremely fortunate to have secured Saint John of the Cross as our speaker for the afternoon, and he has offered to address us on the subject of—' a glance at her notes, made several weeks ago whilst conversing with the speaker by telephone, '—on the subject of the Dark Side of the Knoll. Over to you, Saint John.'

She sits amid a patter of applause.

Saint John of the Cross, looking and sounding faintly irritable, half stands, pushes the hair back from his forehead, and addresses the club president *sotto voce*.

'Er, excuse me, sorry, actually it's not the Dark Side of the Knoll. That sounds like the back of some gloomy little hill. It's actually the Dark Night of the Soul.'

Mrs Stamford-Jones, unperturbed and still smiling proprietorially, rises to her feet once more.

'Sorry, everybody, silly me. Right! Saint John of the Cross speaking on the Dark Side of the Soul.'

'No – no, it's not. It's not the Dark *Side* of the Soul, it's the Dark Side of – wait a minute, I can't remember what it is myself now – oh, yes, that's it, it's the Dark Night of the

Soul. The Dark Night of the Soul. Right?'

Mrs Stamford-Jones' smile remains intact, if a trifle rigid. Although getting on in years now, she's a retired infant teacher who has dealt with any number of awkward children just like Saint John of the Cross in her classes over the years. She intones with patient precision. 'Saint John of the Cross, speaking on the Dark Night of the Soul.'

Saint John of the Cross opens his mouth to speak.

'Is there slides?' The dispassionate query arises from somewhere in the audience.

'No!' Saint John of the Cross is very close to losing it in a big way. 'No, there is – I mean there *are* no slides. I do not *do* slides! I'm a contemplative and mystic who has been divinely vouchsafed insight into an extremely complex and profound phase in the spiritual development of the Christian soul, and I do not – repeat *not* do slides!'

After a short, shocked pause the dispassionate voice is heard again.

'Ooh – cross by name, cross by nature! It's like that Julian man from East Anglia who turned out to be a woman and come to speak to us last year. Got ratty when I said what she was on about boiled down to all's well that ends well. Not sure I want to do this Dark Noel thing if you end up like this bloke.'

Saint John of the Cross, who now sees his future as one of those clowns with the huge check trousers, big red noses and enormous boots, finds his voice rising to an undignified, hysterical squawk. 'Look, it's not something you *do* like going up the gym! I can't possibly talk about it in 15 minutes. It's a very serious and meaningful state of being, and it involves – oh, what's the use? I'm giving it up anyway. Anyone know where the nearest circus is…?'

No, on reflection, I'm more than content to do the little bit of adapting that I have to. And I do rather like cake.

I follow Jesus because …
he's a stickler for accuracy and truth

One of the most sublime experiences of my whole life was hearing my wife ask an elderly French farmer whether it might be possible at some time in the future for her to rent a small strip of his bedroom. She went on to point out with great earnestness that such an arrangement would cause little inconvenience because she would ensure that a small but attractive fence was erected between her section and his. The old Frenchman frowned and scratched his head in bewilderment at this bizarre proposal, lacking, as he did, the essential extra item of information that Bridget, whose French is usually very good (and much better than mine) had got mixed up between the French words for 'field' and 'bedroom'. Truth overcoming gallantry compels me to report that the look of relief on the face of the elderly Frenchman as he realized that a mistake had been made illuminated his granular features like the sun coming up over the French Alps.

It's so easy to make mistakes. Here's another example.

Our last minister was about to move on to take up a different post. An interesting slip of the tongue occurred as he was celebrating his final Holy Communion at the church where Bridget and I worship. It was rather an emotional occasion, of course, and I know from personal experience that when an excess of feeling creeps into any formal proceedings, it's possible to tie oneself in verbal knots with even the most familiar words and phrases. I don't know if I was the only one who noticed this particular example of the genre, but it was, in any case, one of those times when mistakes really don't matter too much.

It happened when the priest was well into that marvellous piece of biblical prose which begins with the words: 'Who in the same night that he was betrayed…'

The bit about the bread went fine, but after that our beloved leader's concentration must have dipped, because he very seriously intoned the following: 'In the same way, after supper he took the cup and gave you thanks; he broke it and gave it to them, saying, 'Drink this, all of you; this is my blood of the new covenant...'

All the regulars would have known perfectly well what he meant to say, of course, but any nonreligious stranger who had chanced to wander in might have been just a little puzzled, to say the least. I found myself reflecting on how lucky we are that Jesus himself managed to be word perfect when it came to these crucial, one-off occasions. The parables would have been told over and over again, so there was little chance of later writers going too far wrong with them, but it wasn't as if they had a Penultimate Supper before the Last one, a sort of dress rehearsal for the real thing. It had to be right first time. Just consider, for one moment, the consequences if Jesus had made the same mistake as our minister.

Every Sunday, in churches all over the world, church leaders of every denominational shade and variety would have found themselves breaking little pieces from a chalice cunningly fashioned out of thin biscuit (or chocolate, perhaps?), dropping them into liquid of some sort, then offering them reverently to members of the congregation, so that they could be drunk in their dissolved state as the Scriptures so mysteriously commanded. There might even have developed a schism between those of the chocolate persuasion and those of the biscuit brotherhood, who were unwilling to expose their members to temptation in such a way.

Irreverent fantasy pictures Jesus paying a surprise visit to one of these churches and scratching his head in bewilderment like that old French farmer on witnessing such strange behaviour.

'Excuse me,' he would tentatively enquire, 'I, er, I was just wondering why you use those – those chocolate cups at Communion.'

'Ah,' would come the confident reply, 'because they dissolve better, of course.'

'They dissolve better?'

'Yes, you know you said we should break the cup and drink it – well, this is the easiest way of doing it.'

'I said what? Oh, dear! I'm most awfully sorry. I meant *take* the cup. And you've been … oh, you haven't, have you? For 2,000 years?'

Son of God collapses in fits of helpless laughter.

A ridiculous scenario? Well, perhaps, but a little thought suggests that we would be very fortunate indeed if the Lord were to react with laughter to all our mistaken habits and practices. The fact is that we in the church have had the greatest difficulty in preserving essential truths that he made perfectly clear and expressed with complete accuracy, so it really is just as well that he wasn't guilty of any verbal errors.

'What?' he might say, as he surveys the church world-wide. 'I distinctly remember making it perfectly clear that you were to love one another. Why have you started a new religion under my name that doesn't just allow but encourages bitter division and unloving conflict? *Why* have you done that? Why?'

'What on earth are these?' he might further ask, as he encounters a succession of dumbly unwelcoming church buildings catering for the sterile religious habits of a few. 'I thought I called you to be fishers of men, not respectable, inward-looking, ignorers of the real world. I told you about the harvest. I was *passionate* about the harvest. Why aren't you out in the fields? People are dying out there! And another thing. Tell me why there are still Pharisees and hypocrites in the church that bears my name, people who continue to put impossible burdens on the shoulders of the men and women I died for, my brothers and sisters who should be free and rejoicing instead of shackled and guilty. Tell me why you put up with them. Tell me now!'

Never mind chocolate chalices and slips of the tongue. The truth is hard enough to handle, but that's what he wants and that's what he's determined to have. I'm glad.

I follow Jesus because ... he doesn't insist that we must all have Scottish accents

One summer morning I was awakened in the early hours by what sounded to my sleep-befuddled brain like a Presbyterian prayer meeting happening in the field behind our house. Getting up quietly so as not to wake Bridget, who deserves her sleep and is in any case a somewhat exclusive Anglican, I peered through the window, half expecting to see a posse of sombre-faced elders petitioning the Lord on the other side of our garden fence. As my eyes grew accustomed to the faint light shed by a handful of stars, it dawned on me that either a number of these pillars of the church community were down on all fours tearing grass up with their teeth like a herd of mad Nebuchadnezzars, or my slumber had actually been disturbed by the flock of sheep that appears in the meadow adjacent to our house at the beginning of each summer.

Lingering by the window, I marvelled at the extraordinarily human sound made by these gentle creatures and the variety of expression possible within the limitations of a simple bleat. Given these two observations, you may ask how I could have believed that a Presbyterian prayer meeting was in progress. Well, it may have been the fact, newly registered at this deeply contemplative moment, that all sheep bleat with a Scottish accent. Now, you may laugh, but consider – isn't it true that every single sheep you have ever heard giving voice, whether in Holland, Israel, New Zealand or Guatemala, has done so with a distinctly Caledonian inflection? I'm right, aren't I?

Jesus likened his followers to sheep for excellent reasons, but might there have been moments during the last 2,000 years when he wished he had chosen a different simile? You can watch the Scottish sheep behind our house cramming themselves into ridiculously inappropriate situations, simply because it feels safer to do what everyone else is doing. This aspect of sheepish behaviour is surely *not* one we're supposed to emulate, yet we do it continually, particularly when it comes to different 'waves' within the church.

A while ago, for instance, I visited a church in the north. Soon after I had taken my seat the woman beside me doubled up, expelling a loud grunt of pain, as though someone had punched her hard in the solar plexus. Deeply alarmed, I asked if she wanted me to get help, but she just smiled beatifically and said, 'Don't worry, love, it's just the Holy Spirit.'

'Just the – oh, I see…'

I didn't see. I was bewildered by my neighbour's explanation of her violent convulsion. I was doubly bewildered when the minister climbed onto the platform at the front and exhibited the same symptoms – only more so. His delivery was so heavily punctuated by 'holy grunts' and clutchings of the stomach that he reminded me of one of those characters being attacked by nobody in films about the Invisible Man. By the end the whole affair was beginning to sound like 30 or 40 heavyweight boxing matches all going on simultaneously. This, apparently, was the way the Holy Spirit had chosen to manifest himself in this particular church. Who was I to argue? People were absolutely sincere about these manifestations. All I can say is that, looking back, I seem to recall a subtle but unmistakably Scottish flavour in those violent utterances.

Passing swiftly over the list of other phenomena spreading like bizarre rashes through our churches in recent years – such things as barking, mooing, laughing, falling over and roaring – we come to the business of dental fillings that miraculously turn to gold.

Our friend was so convinced by a visiting speaker that the fillings of all those present had turned to gold, that she publicly testified to the miracle having happened in her own mouth. Later, after asking a very good friend to inspect her fillings closely, she returned to the church, apologized for getting carried away, and withdrew her testimony.

Set against this is the fact that we once met an evangelist from South America who appeared to have genuinely experienced this strange work of God at a time when it really mattered to him as an individual.

And this must be the important point. God will do *anything* that's truly necessary for any one of his followers at the particular time when that person needs it. Problems arise when the special experience of person A is slavishly copied or imitated by the entire alphabet of other persons in the church because they're frightened of being left out or left behind. How much of what God offers me do I miss because I conform and imitate without really thinking?

Let us love the flock and enjoy being part of it, because that's certainly what Jesus wanted, but let us also be glad that God is, was, and ever will be creatively ingenious in his dealings with individual men and women. I find that very exciting. Do you find that exciting? Are you going to follow me slavishly in finding that exciting?

And all God's people said, 'B-a-a-a-a-a-h!'

I follow Jesus because ...
he takes responsibility for problems
I haven't got a hope of solving on my own

We have more and more palatial shopping precincts in this country, but still no sign of a Wisdom shop. I wish there was somewhere where you could buy wisdom. There are times when I feel sadly lacking in that commodity. The Bible says God will give us wisdom if we need it, and I do believe that, but some situations are so taxing that we can easily lose awareness of the Holy Spirit touching what we do and say.

Here's just one example.

One day I was at my desk, busily writing Bible notes, when – yes, you guessed it – the jolly old phone rang. Now, before I tell you about the phone call, I should explain that these Bible notes related to the first book of Corinthians, chapters four to eight, in which Paul has much to say to the unholy church at Corinth about sin, sex, immorality, divorce, getting married, not getting married, and all that sort of thing. My mind was awash with thoughts and feelings about the conflict between carnality and holiness, and Paul's way of dealing with it in this particular case. It was as I completed note number nine out of fourteen that the phone did its invariable thing.

My caller was a friend (I shall call him George) who for some years has been the highly regarded leader of a large English-speaking church in one of the smaller European countries. I have known George and his wife Martine for many years and, as well as having great respect for their joint ministry, I'm very fond of them both. George sounded very subdued.

'I'm calling to tell you,' he said, 'that I've resigned from my church, and that Martine and I and the children have moved to a different city.'

I groaned inwardly on hearing these words. What disaster could have overtaken my friends?

George cleared his throat uneasily before continuing to speak.

'You see, Adrian, I've been secretly having an affair with someone in the church for over a year now, and the other day it all came out in the open. As a result we've moved right away, and I've been lucky enough to find temporary employment, but at the moment I just can't decide what to do. Poor Martine spends most of the time swinging from sobbing grief to wild anger, and I – well, I feel terribly guilty, but all I want is to be with this woman who's made me feel alive for the first time in years.' He paused for a moment. 'I really do need to come and speak with you, if it's possible.'

'Well, of course,' I responded, trying not to allow the shock I was feeling to sound too much in my voice. The marriage of George and Martine had seemed one of the few still points in a tumultuously turning world. 'Of course you must come if it would help.'

'I'm so glad you said that,' he replied, clearing his throat nervously again, 'because I'm already here.'

'You're already—'

'Just down the road in a phone box. I got the early ferry. I hope you don't mind.'

I told him to come on up to the house, and put the phone down in a state of considerable shock. This minister of the gospel, my friend George, had committed adultery, yearned to continue committing adultery, and would be with me in minutes to talk about it. There, on the desk in front of me, lay the notes I had been making, and the Bible I had been using, still open at the book of Corinthians. I stared at them. George's situation was not theoretical, it was real, and he would be here at any moment. What would I say to him when he arrived? Where did my duty lie? What would Jesus have said? What did he want *me* to say?

I found myself mentally rehearsing different ways of responding to George when he arrived. The voice of my early evangelical upbringing suggested the following: 'You know perfectly well, George, that adultery is against the will of God. The clear path of obedience that lies before you now is one of complete repentance and a new commitment to Martine and the divinely approved marriage that your sinful indulgence has threatened.'

Paul would approve of me saying something along those lines, surely, and there could be no divine comeback later, as far as I was concerned. It was the truth, after all, wasn't it? Was it? I shook my head and sighed. No, it was only a form of truth, truth without a heart, without compassion or understanding. Who was I to tell someone else what they ought to think or do?

Maybe I ought just to create space for George to make his own decisions. Something of this sort: 'George, you have to follow your own heart. The most important thing is to be true to yourself, as the Bible says – no, as you were, it was Shakespeare who said that, wasn't it? Still, same sort of thing – just know what it is you really want, and go for it with all your heart until you've got it. Be the authentic you, whatever anyone else says.'

Paul certainly wouldn't approve of that, I thought, and, to be honest, neither would I, really. I didn't want George to go off with this woman and leave Martine and the children behind. I wanted him to be strong and obedient and to discover that, if he was, God would support him. I wanted – well, mainly I wanted to avoid saying or not saying the very thing that might mess up God's best plan for solving the problem.

I said a prayer: 'Lord, I feel useless and troubled as my friend gets nearer and nearer to my front door. At the moment, I really don't know what to say to him, but there are some things that I do know. I know that Jesus always dealt with people according to their individual circumstances, and that he reacted in ways that were quite surprising and unexpected as far as onlookers were concerned. I know that Jesus only did what he saw the Father doing, rather than using fixed rules or methods. I know that he could be very tender with repentant sinners and very tough with people whose hearts were hardened, and, perhaps most importantly, he could always tell the difference. And I know that you love George and Martine and want the very best for them. Please give me as much of the mind of Christ as I'm capable of making space for, so that I open my mouth and shut it again at the right times. Amen.'

The actual substance of my subsequent conversation with George isn't terribly relevant. I still felt inadequate and lacking in wisdom as we spoke, but I also felt that I had truly released responsibility for my friends to the only one capable of making a real difference. That seemed important to me.

Do say a prayer for all those couples who are facing similar problems.

I follow Jesus because ...
he offers hope for the future

Just before the millennium someone invited me to address a meeting on the subject of 'Hope for the Future'. The organizers suggested that I might like to talk about how the Christian faith enables me to look with hope and serenity to the future, as far as my children and grandchildren are concerned. As I said in my response to their invitation, there are problems with this proposition as it stands.

First, there are major difficulties with the whole idea of Christians being filled with hope and serenity. Contrary to what some shiny-eyed enthusiasts might claim, the Holy Spirit doesn't issue regulation hope-and-serenity kits to all new believers when they turn up at the divine quartermaster's store. Living out the Christian life – actually following Jesus – can be a tough and perilous business, and it certainly offers no earthly guarantees. In the course of his work for God, the apostle Paul experienced many harsh discomforts, including hunger, beatings, shipwreck, imprisonment *and* despair. As far as we can tell, he was more than happy to endure all those things as long as Christ was being preached. Read his letters and his speeches in Acts, and you will see that he was full of hope in the power of the resurrection to save men and women for an eternity with Jesus, and serenely confident that the Holy Spirit would lead him along the right paths to make that possible, but in terms of comfort and physical safety – well, anything could happen.

I certainly don't have Paul's faith and perseverance, but I do think that his priorities were absolutely right, and that's why I look to the future for my children and grandchildren with a mixture of hope and fear. I want them to love Jesus as Paul did, and therefore have the same priorities as him, but I have to confess that my heart almost fails me when I think of the hardship that such a commitment might involve for them. I ask God to give them wisdom, strength, and a love for him so great that it overcomes all obstacles. You see, as I said right at the beginning of this book, I want to be with them in heaven, just as, for instance, I look forward to one day being reunited with my own mother, whom I mentioned earlier. She's the second thing I would like to talk about, because it was her death in particular that enabled me to focus on the priority of eternity in a new and spiritually energizing way.

My mother died towards the end of 1996, and my wife and I found it very hard to come to terms with our loss. To be honest, we didn't want to come to terms with it too quickly. Bridget regarded her mother-in-law as her best friend and so, in many ways, did I. These things always need to take the proper amount of time. But it was so *sad* that we could no longer jump in the car and drive up from Hailsham to Tunbridge Wells to spend a morning or an afternoon with my generous, stubborn, accepting mother. Every now and then I momentarily forgot that she was no longer there, and the words, 'Let's pop up and see Mum,' were on the tip of my tongue. Then I would remember, and the sadness would flood in again. Bridget experienced exactly the same thing. There really is no easy way around grief. You just have to go straight through the middle of it and, for a time at least, accept pain as a constant companion.

One of the saddest things about the death of a close family member is the business of going through their possessions, sorting things into different piles and categories to be thrown away, or sold, or taken home, or given to friends of the person who has died. It felt like a sort of sacrilege to be taking the furniture of Mum's life apart in that way, especially when it came to the things that would be valueless to anyone else but meant a great deal to her. One of the most poignant examples of this was a brochure brought back from a voyage on the *Queen Elizabeth II*. All her life Mum had dreamed of taking a cruise on the famous passenger ship, and finally she had managed to afford a very short trip from the French coast back to England. That glossy brochure was the symbol of a dream fulfilled, and Bridget was about to drop it into one of the black rubbish bags when she stopped and said, with a little catch in her voice, 'I can't throw this away. I know it's silly, but it meant so much to Mum.' We took it home and put it in the cupboard in our bedroom. Mum would laugh at such sentimentalism, that's for sure.

It was strange to see the house eventually completely clear of any trace of the person who had lived there. The accumulated possessions of more than 70 years had been bagged, bought, bequeathed or binned within the space of about three days. All that was left was a shell, as empty of the person who had once inhabited it as the body that I had sat next to for a few minutes after my mother finally gave up the battle for life on earth and went to meet her God.

The sadness involved in disposing of her possessions and the grief over her death would rage with wild meaninglessness if I didn't have the confidence that she has gone to be with Jesus, and that we shall see her again.

But for you who revere my name, the sun of righteousness will rise with healing in its wings. And you will go out and leap like calves released from the stall.

(Malachi 4:2 NIV)

This Old Testament verse provides us with a graphic picture of the experience my mother will have had immediately after her death. *We* may be sad, but I can assure you that she is not. After spending four tedious, frustrating years in a wheelchair, don't you think that being able to leap like a calf released from its stall must be a heavenly pleasure? If you have ever seen calves when they're first released after being confined, you will know that they bounce more or less vertically into the air. They go boing! boing! around their pasture as though they're on springs instead of legs. Healed in the sunshine and leaping for joy. I wish Mum was here, but I'm glad she's there.

There are countless numbers of people all over the world who have never heard of Jesus, let alone learned to revere him as this passage teaches us we must. My mother didn't leave much behind, but her faith, the most valuable asset in her possession, went with her. My prayer and hope is that my children and their children will be part of God's work in bringing those people to the same faith, because nothing is more important. I honestly don't feel very serene about it, but my hope is in Jesus, and if we follow him he will not fail us or them.

I follow Jesus for reasons that are almost impossible to explain

I had to add this last little section because it may be more important than any of the others, and yet I hardly know how to write it. I must, though.

You see, it all falls apart sometimes. The whole thing just crumbles and turns to dust. I don't mind admitting it any more, because I know now that I can only be the me that God has called, just as you can only be you. Sometimes a sad darkness comes and for a little while I can't see my faith in front of my face. When I'm rescued from that darkness, it's not by glib statements, nor by the light of technical theology, but by the living memory of those rare, wonderful, insubstantial, essential, fleeting moments when, in a world where faith and doubt are equally irrelevant, I have simply known that he's there, that he loves me, and that there are important things to be done.

After all, what is Christianity but God driving a jalopy to work with a smile on his face?

Thank you for reading this book.